Video Games and Interactive Media

Video Games
and
Interactive Media

A Glimpse at New Digital Entertainment

Stéphane Natkin

with a foreword by André-Marc Delocque-Fourcaud

Translated by Eric Novak

A K Peters, Ltd.
Wellesley, Massachusetts

Editorial, Sales, and Customer Service Office

A K Peters, Ltd.
888 Worcester Street, Suite 230
Wellesley, MA 02482
www.akpeters.com

This book is based on the book *Jeux vidéo et médias du XXIe siècle* originally published in French by Vuibert, Paris, 2004.

Library of Congress Control Number: 2006921309

ISBN 13: 978-1-56881-297-7
ISBN 10: 1-56881-297-3

Printed in the United States of America
10 09 08 07 06   10 9 8 7 6 5 4 3 2 1

This book is dedicated to the memory of

my brother Gerold,

and

Laurent Herbretau,

one of the founders of the School of Games

Contents

Foreword
Nausicaä's Ball

Some young girls laugh and play on a white beach, and one of them runs to retrieve the ball of woven straw which rolls on the sand. She stifles a frightened cry: a man is sprawled out in the receding waves, completely nude. Soon after, washed, anointed, perfumed, and revived by the spectacle of the nymphs, the shipwrecked voyager will tell his story and give his name: Ulysses. It is the beginning of the Odyssey and the birth of fiction, the first flashback, "Muse, lend me thy lyre," when, as evening falls, the community gathers around the blind poet. I love that this tale, the very first, begins with the game of the nymphs. And did not Greek mythology in fact embrace both Apollo and Dionysus, the rational principle energized by enthusiasm and ecstasy?

Thousands of years later, a constantly increasing number of people take part in a society where work, creation, and the delivery of love letters, family photos and layoff notices are all accomplished with the help of a single machine, a single screen, a single keyboard. A hybrid prosthesis issuing from the improbable union of the great inventions of the two previous centuries: photography, the typewriter, the calculator, the telephone, the phonograph, cinema, radio, and television, all united by the first common language of the community of mankind: bits and bytes. The Tower of Babel finally completed, in noise, blood, and furor.

Will it astonish us for much longer that the fascinating and formidable triumph of this tool, which both liberates and enslaves us, has so quickly elicited its Dionysian partner? This is the adventure which Stéphane Natkin relates to us, that of the game, improperly qualified by the word "video," today more properly called digital and interactive.

Thus, the poet, the composer, the system administrator, or the accountant may, with a simple "click," pass from the Apollonian mode to the Dionysian mode, without leaving—moving from constraint to diversion, or from ecstasy to laughter—their aptly named "workstation." It is a revolution, yet another one. Stéphane Natkin tells us its engrossing history. A history whose primitive age doesn't reach beyond thirty years and which is still being written, before our eyes and on our screens.

This sensational eruption of the game into the computer, of the Dionysian world into the world of Apollo, is rich with another promise. A game is interactive by nature, from the very first ball exchanged between Nausicaa and her companions on that original white beach. Fiction is only slightly so. The songs of the poet, the imprecations of tragedians, the vocalizations of opera, and the theoretically complete spectacle offered by "cinematic theater" all confront the emotions of a passive public, which on its own side can only communicate by applauding.

A question arises immediately. Does not the video game promise an artistic revolution: interactivity in fiction? At present, it still attempts this imperfectly, but with constant progress—through role-playing games, strategy games, and piloting simulations for various real or imaginary machines. Let us not feign innocence; we know very well where we're going: a fiction in which we shall not only be spectators but also heroes; the terminus—surely provisory—of humanity's long quest from the beach of Nausicaa towards the art of evasion, of the identification of the spectator/player with the hero/character, to the point of influencing his destiny, of becoming his own author. All of this with the requirements of triumphing over obstacles, of defeating adversaries, of knowing how to be helped, how to be loved by one's friends. In brief, the requirement of taking care of the Other, just as in real life.

It is to this very adventure that the new century delivers us. Let us stipulate that this stuttering art and spectacle, whose origins Stéphane Natkin speaks of, shall have become a major art form well before the century finishes. Let us dare to imagine that this "cinema/game," within the borders outlined in the work we are about to read, shall be *the* art of the twenty-first century, just as cinema was that of the twentieth. After all, in 1904, we were at *The Assassination of the Duke de Guise*, and cinema has made some progress since then.

I suffocate, exhausted, blinded, deafened in the waves and sand. Around me, the water retreats. An apparition looks at me, a beautiful young woman, richly tanned in her short tunic, ready to take flight, as frightened as I am. I stutter my name: Ulysses.

André-Marc Delocque-Fourcaud
Director of the National Center of
the Comic Strip and the Image, Angoulême
March 2004

Preface

This book began as a manifesto for the creation of a master's degree in video-game design and, later, the establishment of the Graduate School of Games and Interactive Media in France (Ecole Nationale des Jeux et Media Interactifs Numériques (ENJMIN, http://www.enjmin.fr/). When this idea of a degree in multimedia design was brought up in discussions with several people from CNAM, La Rochelle University, Poitiers University, and CNBDI (National Center for Comic Strips and Images) in 1997, my only connection to video games was my 12-year-old son, Renaud, who could spend hours in front of a TV set playing video games while I tried to take him out for some physical exercise. Quickly, Pascal Estraillier, professor and director of the computer research center at La Rochelle University, suggested focusing our training program on video games. I started to investigate what exactly video games are and how they are designed, manufactured, and marketed. With Cecile Le Prado, the head of the sound department at ENJMIN, I went from studio to studio and from publisher to publisher to conduct interviews with people who worked on games on a daily basis. These efforts had a major effect on my life. I became an active player myself. One cannot analyze and teach video games without playing them. As a side effect. I found that I enjoy playing them. Later, I became the head of a research group working on game-design theory, intelligent interfaces for games, interactive sound and music, and much more. Finally, I became fascinated by the world of games and the people who make them.

In this book, I try to provide a rationale for the creation of graduate-level programs in game design. Along the way, I will give a justification for my fascination with games and their importance in the evolution of our society. One of the main changes in our civilization over the last century is the development of communication networks: telephone, radio, and television. The consequences of this development are tremendous. As individuals, we have completely changed our way of communicating. Globally, the omnipresence of broadcast and other mass media has facilitated intercultural exchange and cross fertilization. To some degree, this has led to the predominance of the American way of life. At the end of the century, the growth of the Internet suggests a new communication revolution relying on interactive media. The big question, as yet unsolved, concerns the type of social interaction and content that will be introduced by interactive networks. It will need a sociological maturation time to close the gap between the development of new technology and the creation of new practices and cultural content.

In an attempt to understand this evolution of media, we focus on one of the most mature and successful areas, considering the market, design, and production practices: the computer-game industry. In terms of sales, the computer-game industry is in third place among other media, after TV and CD plus DVD, and before movie ticket sales. In contrast to the chaos of the design of the Web, the game industry and, more specifically, game designers have rather clear ideas on what a computer game is, its audience, and the design and production process. They have, in our opinion, defined a new genre of audiovisual production even if one has to admit that, as of now, there are only a few computer-game masterpieces.

It is interesting to note that technology developed in the context of computer games is being exported to other areas. This is true for programming techniques, hardware and software innovation in imaging and sound, distributed computing and networking (used in massively multiplayer online games (MMOGs)), education ("serious games" and simulation used in professional and military training) and medical (psychiatric) therapy. Work on games and learning has constantly increased since the famous work of the MIT Media Lab in 1996. Major projects in the US (Prensky, 2001), Canada (Kaufman, 2005), Europe, and Japan are focused on this subject, the main purpose of which is not to include tricky games in online training systems but to understand what can be learned by playing and transforming the game-design immersion and learning techniques into pedagogical principles and tools. Many commercial games are already used as an advertising medium: you can

A digital library interface relying on the RenderWare game engine
(Dupire, 2005).

find McDonald's restaurants in *The Sims,* and Sony uses the billboards
in its football games to promote its own consoles. Moreover, the purpose of some persistent worlds is mainly advertising (Book, 2005). In
the last chapter of this book, we present the technology of persistent online games. The development of this technology needs to solve some of
the most difficult problems of distributed computing. Hence, if someone is able to manage a real-time persistent universe where thousands of
gamers are interacting, he is also able to provide tools for almost all the
online collaborative work applications. For example, he can build a virtual stock exchange (Favier, 2004) or a virtual university with thousands
of students.

The design of games is a rather difficult task. As in other par-
ticipatory works, the author must leave a controlled freedom to the
client/audience. But, as opposed to art installations or interactive music
composition, the game industry is driven by marketing goals. Games are
mainly entertainment; hence, the player must solve nontrivial but not
too complex problems, leading to a succession of goals in a reasonable
amount of time. The player must feel as if he is in an open interactive

work but should be driven to the game solution. To solve this dilemma, the game industry has invented several techniques borrowed from game theory and object-oriented programming. The feeling of immersion is explicitly the main goal of game narrative. To increase the feeling of immersion, game design is a subtle mix of three domains. The first two are directly related to linear storytelling and cinema: dramatic principles of scenario design (tension and climax) and qualities of the visual and sonic universe. The third inherits from classical games: challenges of gameplay. We believe that these techniques are the source of a new fundamental approach to interactive narration. It is, as of now, mainly a practice, but we see a new theory, based on the understanding of actual games, being developed (Glassner, 2004], [Salem, 2004].

Multiplayer games have other goals: the main interest of the player is the development of new social relations, so the work of the designer is to define rules and stories that lead to socialization. In MMOGs, thousands of players meet and share a persistent virtual society whose rules are initially defined by the game designers but which evolve with the demand of the player community. The designer of an MMOG needs to create a virtual but operational universe with all its physical, economic, and social components. If you want to become a god, design online games. But also, if you want to understand the essence of next-generation interactive television programs, look at MMOGs and consider it as a broadcast media where each spectator has his own camera and is able to interact with other participants.

The history of the Internet, from chatrooms to blogs, has demonstrated the potential for each individual to be a source of information (and disinformation), fiction, and art. Game technology introduces some new features in the production of homemade multimedia. Game modification (mod) editors allow the use of the game engine to modify the game objects and even some of the game rules. This leads to either a new game (the very popular multiplayer game *Counter-Strike* is a mod of the game *Half-Life*) or something that is an art installation or a virtual meeting room. Then if you record a game session with a virtual camera, you can be the director of a film with characters and sets that you designed. Such digital productions are becoming more and more popular on the Internet. Some commercial games, like *The Sims 2* or *The Movies*, provide all the tools needed to produce such multimedia. Some

http://babeltivi.free.fr

BABEL TiVi © Martin WELTER, Stéphanie DE BIASIO, Vivien CHAZEL

BabelTV, a video-game proposal for interactive television (ENJMIN Project, 2005).

remarkable short films have been produced this way in the last two years. One of the members of a guild in an MMOG recorded a documentary of a hopeless six-month quest of his guild in the virtual world. A story about the riots in France in November 2005 (*The French Democracy*) was produced in three weeks using the game *The Movies*. Combining this ability to produce animations with the fact that many people can record events using digital-video capabilities included in mobile phones and digital cameras will probably change the TV production environment. Some Web TV channels are already relying on works created by their audience.

MMOGs use "classical" ten-year-old technology. New concepts and devices are changing the scene. We think about mobile and ubiquitous computing, tangible interfaces, smart devices, etc. The next-generation media will rely on the cross-media uniform platform. The principle is rather simple: the user may interact with the same interactive virtual world using many kinds of devices, such as home-theater systems, computers, interactive TV sets, PDAs, mobile phones, and any intelligent object including sensors and actuators. The media interface will be automatically adapted to the device. A rather simple (and poor) vision of this platform is the automatic transformation of a web page from a computer interface to a mobile-phone interface. A much more advanced concept of the unified platform can be thought of in terms of new content creation, in particular, for the next generation of games. The most advanced feature of the unified platform would be the ability to mix passive broadcast media and interactive media into a unified whole.

To understand the impact of these technologies, consider the increasingly complex relationships between the real world and the virtual world, in multiplayer games and, more generally, in entertainment applications. The following examples are developed later in this book.

- It is well known that MMOGs have complex economic systems and that some of the virtual goods produced can be sold on the real market, having a direct impact on the real economy.

- Proactive games like *Majestic* or *In Memoriam* use email and the phone to interact asynchronously with the current activity of the player. It was probably the first clever approach of "push" fiction in media.

- Mobile-phone localization is already used to facilitate the meeting of multiplayer gamers. In advanced applications, there is a mapping between the topology of the virtual world and the topology of the real one: players are searching for virtual treasures in real towns.

- Augmented-reality games use real space and time as the framework of an adventure, where virtual characters appear through mobile interfaces such as goggles.

- There have already been several attempts to use real-time events (sports, variety shows, and even political events) broadcast through media such as radio and TV as the background of a game played on an interactive TV set.

Players collaborating in *Human Pac-Man,* an augmented-reality game (Cheock, 2004).

More generally, these examples foresee the development of a new generation of interactive media using both real and virtual worlds in a complex mixed mode, and games are the front line of this evolution.

From the previous discussion, one may see a world of games as a dream. It can also be a nightmare. From my point of view, the danger is not related to violence or immorality in games: games are not different from other media. If a society is able to develop a critical analysis of games, it is able cope with this danger. Addiction to games has been observed, and several psychologists and sociologists have analyzed this new kind of drug. We will come back to this subject later, but it seems that game addiction is a threat for psychologically weak people, and it is maybe less dangerous to be addicted to online games than to cocaine. Going back to our analysis and the relationship between games and media, we see the danger elsewhere. Game design and game artificial intelligence rely on a subtle analysis of player behavior. In this book, we will show that the level of analysis of player psychology and sociology is the main original contribution to game-design principles. A game is created to satisfy the player's needs, however you define this word:

a feeling of freedom, lust for power, seduction, etc. A game, as an extension of existing mass media, alters the feeling of reality, leading to a view of the world that always satisfies the player/spectator. The danger is the use of this knowledge to control customer habits, moral attitudes, or political viewpoints. The art of game design is at its first stage; it can become the basis of new techniques of mass manipulation. It can also be the technology of an intelligent augmented-reality world, where this technology helps people to live and creates new things. Like other media, it can lead to the best and the worst things. The best, and maybe the only, way to prevent the danger is to understand it and then teach clever people all the aspects of video games and their evolution.

This book is organized as follows. The first chapter tries to define what a video game is. The problem is not as simple as it seems. After a brief history of video games, we describe the game production process and economy. The second chapter is devoted to single-player game-design principles. Its goal is not to describe in detail the state of the art in game design but to show that the current practices and theory introduce new concepts in entertainment and narration. The third chapter analyzes persistent and ubiquitous games as an anticipation of new mass media. The fourth chapter is a review of the state and evolution of game technologies. In the fifth chapter, we discuss the possible emergence of a new art form based on game principles.

Acknowledgments

This book is the outcome of the cooperative, multiplayer game which resulted on the one hand in the creation of the master's program at the School of Video Games and Interactive Media, and on the other hand in a research program under the direction of the laboratories CEDRIC and L31. The winning team resulted from a coalition of teachers and researchers coming from the universities of la Rochelle, of Poitiers, of the CNAM Paris, of the CNAM Poitou-Charentes, of the CNBDI, and of the IRCAM. I would therefore like to thank its members: Viviane Gal, Sophie Pierson, Liliana Vega, Françoise le Vézu, Chen Yan, Jean Michel Blottière, Thierry Bouwmans, Pierre Cubaud, Jérome Dupire, Pascal Estraillier, Jean Marc Farinone, Eric Gressier-Soudan, Françoise Guercin, Alexandre Topol, and Jose Xavier. A particular word of thanks goes to André-Marc Delocque-Fourcaud, who agreed to give this book a mythological preface. I cannot forget my teammate Cécile Le Prado. Having entered into the match without knowing the rules of the game, she was able to create a unique pedagogical approach to sound in video games.

Finally, and above all, I am also very thankful to all of the students, whose passion, creative abilities, and intellectual curiosity are some of the incomparable elements of gameplay. Many illustrations in this book are taken from their projects (see table). Each group retains the copyright for the project concept, realization, sound, and images.

I was able to dedicate so much time to this project, which might seem a bit odd from the viewpoint of higher education, thanks to the understanding of the administration and of my colleagues at the National Conservatory of Arts and Professions, Paris, who have keenly perceived the issues hidden behind Rayman's fists and Lara Croft's pistols.

I would also like to thank the team at A K Peters who has taken a lot of time to develop this book in the complex relationship between a French author and an American publisher.

Project Name	Year	Student Names
Fin de l'ancien temps	2002	*Y. Chapus*, T. Dilger, V. Moreews, C. Vercruysse
Genetik Warriors	2002	C. Bedel B. Cheret, N. Darsot, *O. Kadi*, S. Navarro, C. Vincent
Poussiéres de Lune	2002	*G. Artus*, S. Chevallier, B. Hubert, B. Mangin, F. Nourry, *N. Serikoff*, J. Tanant, *S. Tisne*
Bugs in Toon	2003	A. Dallemagne, *E. David*, A. Gaudin, T. Gaudy, J. Gregoire, A. Levêque, S. Pluu
Eoliane	2003	M. Barnaud, C. Fanfan, T. Fontin, T. Gaudy, T. Pasquier, S. Scherrer, P. Seguinau
Hot Spital	2003	J.Barrois, E. Bréchémier, E. Carré, H. Dintinger, G. Macerot, J. Naulin, E. Sabatié, K. Seng, E. Thoa, A. Vaudour, S. Confoulan
Les terres d'IA	2003	A. Bauzat, G. Chavaroche, T. Ferreira, D. Lechat, *P. Meggeville*, N. Sejourne, E. Sablon, R. Soulier
Nano Futur	2003	*A. Checkroun*, E. Boutry, B. Detavernier, A. Gaudin, C. M. Lopes, *S. Moussa*, T. Potin
Shadow Run	2003	N. Brault, J. Friedlander, *C. Latour*, C. Lopes, V. Percevault, L. Ruaud , A. Thion, V. Vimont
Children of The Sun	2004	C. Chambon., S. Diaz , L. *Duliscouët*, N. Guillotin, S. Varrault, A.Vaudour, O. Veneri, F. Wolf
Kitchen Frenzy	2004	*P. Alessio*, C. Bartez, X. Collet, A. July, E. Thomas, N. Magenesse, C. Panattoni, E. Thoa,
Swarm	2004	S. Cheam, *T. Foucher*, D. Goumard, B. Gros, J. Lafont, J. Leroux, J. Rousse, P. Strelezki
Wanted	2004	S. Confoulan, N. Gauthier, H. Idjouadiene, A. Monbet, C. Langlois, *G. Penotet*, H. Quach
Addiction	2005	M. Brunem, O. Adelh, A. Roy

Student projects. (Names of graphic designers are in italics.)

Project Name	Year	Student Names
Babel TiVi	2005	V. Chaze, S. de Biasion, M. Welter
Blindway	2005	J. Derrien, H. Dufour, L. Kargul, J. Sinn,
Bob Pop	2005	X. Brisbois, B. Jacqmier, R. Morado, S. Regnault
Citadelles	2005	X. Dauchy, D. Elahee, B. Huet, X. Sadoulet
Colorama	2005	M. Hector, S. Hénot, L. Lavigne, C. Larribal, M.Petit, B. Vimont,
Diodrama	2005	P. Guitton, I. Caroulle, E. Raud, J. Bourbonnais
Last Person	2005	M. Auer, M. Manier, J. Molteni, T. Paulev, G. Reymonenq, M. Tomkinson
Le jardin de Mirabelle	2005	S. De Biasio, *E. Raud*, A Roy, *A. Seghezzi*, J. Spielmann, A. Vegara
Legend of Jia Ling	2005	*X. Hou*, S. Huyn, O.Lee, P. Louvel, *A. Seghezzi*

Student projects, continued. (Names of graphic designers are in italics.)

- 1 -

On the Nature of Video Games

Introduction

In this chapter, we set the stage for the fantasy world of video games. We begin by proposing a definition of what a video game is, and we outline a gaming zoology. This is not a simple question: it will be revisited in the later chapters of this book. We then give a short history of video games and a taste of the economics and production processes of current games. In the preface to this book, we asserted that the video game is the most advanced sector within the domain of interactive media. At the end of this chapter, the reader may think that this is an uncultivated and immature world. This is certainly true, but in the realm of the blind, the one-eyed man is king.

A Zoology of Gaming

Introduction

What is a video game? There are many possible answers to this question. On the one hand, the only practical relation that video games have with video is in the nature of the signal transmitted between the console and the monitor. It would perhaps be more appropriate to speak of computer games. On the other hand, this term covers a range of objects which are used in widely varying conditions. The classic picture of a solitary player in front of a console or dedicated PC, dueling with

1

a dragon, only covers a small part of the world of video games. In a *LAN*[1] *party*, a group of players gathers in one room to play out, at the keyboard or in front of a console, a hybrid between a game of cowboys and Indians and a team sport, which tires only the thumb and index finger. Massively multiplayer games assemble communities of thousands of people who find themselves, through the Internet, in a virtual world where the supermarket cashier is a prince and his boss is a serf. Let's not forget the children, from age 7 to 77, in a bus or a subway, plugged into their Game Boys, personal digital assistants, or mobile phones for a round of bug jumping or alien shooting. At the other end of the world, Japanese teens gather in gigantic halls for frantic dances performed on hundreds of interactive mats, to the beat of a manga techno. Network games on mobile phones, already widely used in Japan and Korea, allow for exchanges, often brief, that lie somewhere between the joys of board games and romantic chat. And, of course, it is possible to blend all of these types of game together.

In this book, the term *video game* refers to an interactive audiovisual work whose primary aim is to entertain its users/spectators, and which uses for its implementation a machine based on computer technology. This definition therefore excludes all those products which use game formats for other ends: teaching and training techniques, a basis or subject of an artistic installation, means of navigating the complex subject of a scientific CD-ROM, selling merchandise on the Internet, etc.

If we impose this limit upon ourselves, it is in order to better put into evidence that which characterizes present-day video-game production in comparison to other forms of electronic publication. However, that which makes up the essential innovation of video games will largely escape this limited framework to integrate itself into new narrative forms and to serve as a model for interactive media.

The element that characterizes a video game is the intervention of a computer. It can play two distinct roles. It is always the machine that manages the game's universe, that fabricates a visual and sonic universe in real time, determined by the game design and by the actions of the players. It is also the computer that applies the rules of the game. In certain cases, and in particular for all single-player games, the computer is also the player's adversary.

---

[1] LAN: local area network.

Alone Against the Machine: Single-Player Games

Several classifications for video games exist, according to historical, editorial, or narrative criteria. The specialized press generally makes a distinction between action, adventure, strategy, and sports games. A more precise classification is given by Le Diberder (Le Diberder, 1998) and discussed by Genvo (Genvo, 2003). That of Rollings (Rollings, 2003) is based both on narrative form and on the principal focus of the player. We will propose a simpler classification, based on the mechanisms within a game, called the *gameplay*, and then discuss this classification.

To understand it, we must start from a rather simple point of view, which we develop in Chapter 2: a game presents a universe in which a player must follow a particular story, out of an ensemble of possibilities. This indeterminism should give the player the sensation of liberty and of responsibility for his choices. These choices should seem complex and irreversible: "a game is a series of interesting choices," according to Sid Meier (Rollings, 2003).

Let us first consider single-player games, in which the player plays against the computer. We distinguish four large classes of games: puzzle games, strategy games, action games, and adventure games.

Puzzle games (in terminology borrowed from Rollings) are the computer versions of "classic" games for several players, in which the computer plays the role of one of the players: go, chess, Monopoly, etc. What characterizes these games is the symmetric position of the player and the computer: both know at the beginning the rules which are imposed on them, and they have symmetric roles. Initially, the puzzle games were designed for play between humans; then, some nice work on artificial intelligence allowed one of the players to be replaced by the computer.

Strategy games give the player the sensation of managing a universe. The game's appeal here resides in the apparent complexity of the rules that govern the virtual universe, and thus in the subtleness of the game's strategies. The player is sometimes a god, sometimes an immortal head of state, sometimes a political administrator, who is in charge, respectively, of souls, an empire, or a town. The sensation of immersion simultaneously combines political ambition, the intellectual challenge which comes with a multiplicity of choices, and the interest of a fictional universe in which these choices are offered. The graphical universe of strategy games derives from the style of maps, a global vision of the universe which may have a god or a great general acting within it.

Settlers IV (Blue Byte Software/Ubisoft, 2001).

An action game is a game whose main focus is the dexterity of the player. "Lots of frantic button pushing," according to A. Rollings. Fighting games, shooting games using diverse weapons, and platform games are some of the archetypes of the genre. Among the many action games, we make note of the FPS (first-person shooter) games *Doom*, *Quake*, and *Halo*. *Rez* is an FPS which takes place in an abstract universe. It has experienced limited commercial success but has gained a reputation for the originality of its soundtrack and its graphics, generated in real time.

Platform games, which have as their main difficulty a journey through an imaginary and obstacle-filled universe, can also be placed in the category of action games. Mario, Sonic, and Rayman are the heroes

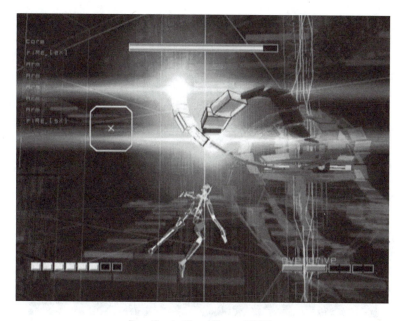

Rez (Sonic Team/Sega, 2001).

of the oldest platform games. Among the fighting games, we mention the well-known games *Tekken*, *Street Fighter*, and *Mortal Kombat*. Dancing games, one of the rare categories which has a female (Japanese or Korean) majority of players, rely on a choreography which the player must follow. They use a specific interface, a dancing mat, which is like a large keyboard operated by the feet.

Adventure games are the most plot-driven—a story wherein the player is the protagonist. A shared feature of these games is an overarching narrative web, together with some rules which draw the player into this web. In order to progress in the adventure, the player must solve certain puzzles or triumph in various action sequences. It is the form that these puzzles and action sequences take which give the sense of freedom and game immersion. However, the essential interest of the game lies in the underlying audiovisual narration. The *Tomb Raider* series of games, known for its famous heroine, Lara Croft, are adventure games that border on action. This category contains numerous subcategories. The survival horror games are counterparts of horror or suspense films.

The *Silent Hill*, *Alone in the Dark*, and *Resident Evil* series are the most popular in this area. In a less gory and more poetic style, *Zelda*, a series

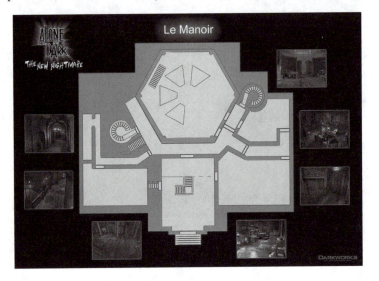

Alone In the Dark 4 (Darkworks/Infogrames, 2001).

created by the famous game developer Shigeru Miyamoto, transports the player to a dream-like world in order to solve various puzzles and defeat rather more decorative monsters. In studies on the subject, one may find many other classes of games mentioned, but from the point of view of gameplay, these are all combinations of the three preceding classes.

The following types are classical mixes of the four basic classes of games.

Individual sports games (snowboarding and other sliding sports, tennis, billiards. golf, car and other vehicle racing, etc.) allow one to be athletic without leaving the couch, and the only risk is a cramp of the wrist.

These have the same basic principles of play as the action games but require a simulation of physical processes, and therefore a greater realism, in order to reproduce well-known forms of competition. An important subcategory of this type of game consists of flight simulators and simulators for the piloting of other vehicles.

Pool Hall Hustle, a sports game on a mobile phone (Lagardere Active North America, 2006).

Flight Simulator X (Microsoft, 2006).

Team sports games (soccer, football, basketball, etc.) retain a focus on the skills needed for individual games, but add a component of team strategy.

The challenge is no longer only physical but also intellectual: the player is simultaneously the forward/center and the coach. The perception of the universe in these games relates to the standard view of the team sport as seen on television.

Pro Rugby Manager (Cyanide Studio, 2005).

Discovery games are the gaming partners of audiovisual documentaries. Through a framework taken from one of the preceding genres, most often that of adventure games, these games present an entire collection of issues which are historical, geographical, ecological, etc., in nature. The French company Cryo, later renamed Dreamcatcher France, is a specialist in this type of game. For example, the games *Versailles* and *Versailles II* present, within a puzzle-solving framework, the discovery of the world of the court of King Louis XIV.

Versailles 2 (Dreamcatcher/RMN, 2001).

In a role-playing game (RPG), the player inhabits a character within an adventure. However, the powers of the character, and thus his ability to progress through the adventure, depend on a complex management system similar to the mechanisms of strategy games. The most famous series of role-playing games is *Final Fantasy*, which in its single-player mode is in its tenth episode.

Action/adventure games, as their name indicates, are adventure games where the principal obstacles that oppose player progress are connected to action sequences (in general, combat). Games focused on infiltration are also included in this category. The player is a spy who must, within the framework of an often complex adventure, work his way through enemy territory as discreetly as possible. Among the famous series in this category we mention *James Bond*, *Metal Gear Solid*, and *Splinter Cell*.

Fahrenheit (Atari/Quantic Dream, 2005).

We shall return to this classification of games in Chapter 2, while studying the different types of gameplay, but we may already connect it to a second criterion used in classification: the length of a match.

Here, a *match* is defined as a session of the game that does not depend on the preceding sessions and that ends with a result correlated to some criterion of player success. There are video games (perhaps more properly called "video toys") that are not played in the form of matches. Some strategy games are ecological, social, or economic in nature and don't have an end, a priori. For example, one must take care of an aquarium, a town, or a small virtual population (as is the case in the well-known series *The Sims*). The length of the game is only limited by the complexity of the simulated universe: when it is too simple, the players will reexperience situations they have already met. In most of these games, there does exist some notion of failure: death of all the fish, destruction of the town, loss of social stability. On the other hand, the notion of success is much more relative: what is a beautiful aquarium, a well-administered town, or a good framework of social politics?

Among the games which do include a notion of match, one may make a distinction between the games with short matches, from a few minutes to a half-hour, and the games whose matches may last for several dozen hours. The short-matched games are generally action games, which are often originally produced as arcade games (played in a gaming arcade on a dedicated system), and subsequently on a PC or console. Since the game is based on the reflexes of the player, the learning of rules is in general quite rapid. One of the focuses of the game is competition, through comparison of the scores obtained by different players. Strategy games and adventure games are based either on rules that are more complex to learn or on a narrative framework. They are thus, in principle, games with long matches. They are either played at home, on a PC or a console, or in a gaming room on a network.

Never Alone In Front of the TV: Multiplayer Games

Multiplayer games make use of the same types of universes as single-player games. A game often offers a single-player mode and a multiplayer mode. One can therefore classify them equally well as strategy games, sport games, adventure games, etc. However, the motivations of the players, and by consequence the gameplay, are often very different. Even if the single-player games have a socializing aspect which often escapes superficial critical analyses, the social aspect is at the very heart of multiplayer games.

A multiplayer game may be either cooperative, where the players play together against the computer, or competitive, where the players play, either alone or on teams, against one another.

In terms of gameplay, cooperative games are an extension of single-player games, adding the dimension of collective effort in order to defeat the machine. Competitive games rely on completely different principles, which render them closer to board games or sports games. The essential difference between the two types of game is contained in the knowledge of the rules. In games played against the computer, the players do not know the exact rules of the game. Control over how the rules are learned is part of the gameplay. The relation between the player (or players in a cooperative game) and the computer is not symmetric. In competitive games, all players must have the same level of knowledge of the rules, even if, in some cases, they accept different roles within the game.

Competitive games have two modalities which we have already mentioned: individual games and team games.

The concept of match, which we developed for single-player games, applies just as well to multiplayer games. Short-matched games may be sports games (automobile racing, for example), action games, or, most often, fighting or shooting games. Games with long matches are strategy games. Games without matches are called persistent games: the game continues to evolve, even when some of the players aren't playing.

Finally, it is necessary to differentiate between games played by open or closed communities. In the first case, the player has no control over the identity of the other people he plays with. In general, the players do not know each other physically and meet via their avatars in the game universe. These are played on the Internet, with communities that are very large, up to many thousands of players. Often, these are role-playing games, called massively multiplayer online role-playing games (MMORPGs). The games with closed communities put into competition a group of individuals or teams who are mutually identified and accepted. When played in a game room, they know each other physically. On the Internet, the players may only know each other through the network. These communities are limited to a dozen or so players.

Games on mobile phones and personal digital assistants are in a stage of rapid development. In single-player mode, they are identical to the games developed for portable consoles like Nintendo DS and Sony PSP, which resemble games on the Nintendo and Sega consoles from ten years ago. The new element here is the use of telephone

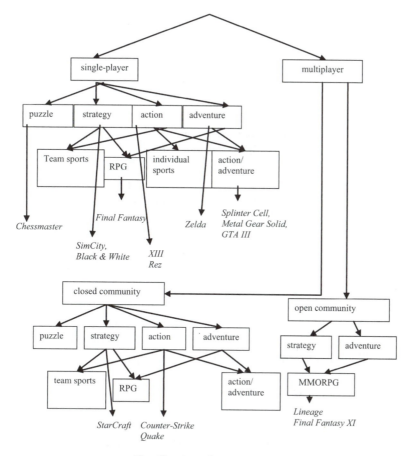

Classification of game types.

and wireless networks to develop games which dynamically assemble small communities. This may result in an electronic renaissance of classic social or board games, with the telephone replacing the deck of cards. Finally, we mention proactive games, which confront the player through telephone or email, and which we will discuss in Chapter 3.

The above figure presents a classification of the principal types of games that may be found in the market, along with the examples that are mentioned in this book. Although some actually exist in more than one mode, these are only cited in the category in which they are referenced in the text.

An Uncultivated Field

The preceding classification is open to discussion and is not founded on a theoretical analysis of gaming narration. We shall return to this point in the next chapter. This is one of the side effects resulting from a lack of critical references for games. The formal analysis of this field has just begun, and there are few works in this area. Nor does there exist a comparative study of different games, in contrast to the vast literature of cinematic analysis. The principal avenue for criticism, with a few exceptions, is either that of the specialized press, which works from the point of view of the basic player, or that of video-game detractors who, having spent an hour in a gaming room observing a complex FPS like Half-Life, have only gathered that everyone shoots at each other. The release of a deeply amoral game, like Grand Theft Auto, which gives the player a role as a small-time thug, has not been conducive to any fundamental analysis. Mechanisms for control over gaming content arise either from self-censorship (game labels supplied by publishers), or from the lobbying of parental and other interest groups who raise a ruckus in the United States. We note finally that, until two or three years ago, the conservation of old games was only done by a few devoted fans. Collections of classic games are now beginning to appear. The French Bibliothèque Nationale manages a game depot; some museums have begun to see the light of day. A bit more effort, and the video game may assert its cultural value.

A Short History of Video Games

There are some works in English (Demaria, 2002) (Kent, 2001) and in French (Le Diberder, 1998) (Ichbiah, 2004), which outline the history of video games. We shall content ourselves here with a short exposé that will allow us to understand the present-day status of games. We are strongly inspired by the presentation given by Alain Le Diberder (Le Diberder, 2003).

According to Le Diberder, the video-game world is in its sixth cycle. Each cycle is characterized by a new technology, a growth in the strength of the sector, and a subsequent collapse containing a preview of the following cycle.

The history starts at the beginning of the sixties, with the appearance of the first computer games, developed by bored physicists or for technological demonstrations. The ancestors of *Pong* and *Spacewar*, invented by a physicist and an electrician, are the fruits of this epoch. At the beginning of the seventies, the necessary technical and economic conditions for the appearance of video games were in place:

- a powerful toy industry;

- television in a great number of living rooms;

- the social use of mechanical games (like pinball) and game arcades;

- the buying power of children and adolescents, which had been developing since the fifties;

- computer technology that no longer served uniquely for business or scientific calculations, but that began to play a role in areas ranging from the control of industrial processes to the treatment of images and sound.

The crucial technological element was the appearance of the microprocessor, commercialized by Intel in 1971. In 1972, Nolan Bushnell created the first video-game company, Atari, and introduced the first electronic arcade game, *Pong*. In less than one year, Atari sold more than 10,000 machines. In 1976, the first console was released, which only played *Pong*, and in 1976, Warner bought Atari for the modest sum of twenty-eight million dollars. The immediate and considerable success of Atari influenced the appearance of a number of contemporary consoles. While Apple was preparing to announce one of the first microcomputers, the Apple II, an abundance of products that quickly became stale put an end, in Christmas 1977, to the first cycle of video games. Nolan Bushnell and Atari remained the principle players in the second episode of the saga. This cycle began with the announcement of the first multi-game console, the Atari VCS 2600, which, through a new spectrum of games produced a renaissance of possibilities for gameplay.

An industry of game publication was born. The totemic game from this epoch is *Pac-Man*, created in Japan by Toru Iwatani for Namco. Atari bought back the license for the VCS, which went on to sell 22 million cartridges. In 1982, Atari's sales figures reached 323 million dollars and delivered a net income of more than twenty million dollars. These numbers, which caused businessmen and speculators to salivate, engendered an overproduction of primarily mediocre games.

The growth of microcomputers and a certain lack of creativity ended up giving game consoles the appearance of outmoded gadgets. Sales fell beginning in 1983. Confronted by losses that quickly became astronomical, Warner resold the Atari activity console to one of the founders of microcomputer producer Commodore, and the arcade-game branch to the Japanese company Namco. The end of video games was announced in the press. In the same epoch, Nintendo, a company which began in the 19th century with the manufacture of card games, and which had already made a fortune by creating little pocket games and arcade games, readied itself to announce the NES console—the Japanese rejoined the party. In less than three months, the NES became all the rage in Japan. This success had three main causes: a price half as big as those of concurrent consoles, a technology that allowed Nintendo to control the games developed for the console and thus to guarantee the quality, and a style of game geared towards eight to ten-year-olds. The iconic hero of the NES and of Nintendo was Mario, a mustached plumber, who began his career by confronting a crazy gorilla, Donkey Kong. His creator, a graphic artist in training, Shigeru Miyamoto, remains a beacon in the dream world of video games.

The third cycle essentially unfolded in Europe and the United States with the development of family microcomputers: Commodore, Sinclair, Amstrad, and, in 1986, the Atari ST, whose release marked the high point of this cycle. These machines allowed the player to play games that were truly innovative in their nature and in their graphic and audio qualities. The landscapes found in each level were different and, within each level, constantly renewed through the sideways scrolling of the screen. The introduction of real-time synthesis enabled a renewal of the soundtrack never before achieved. These microcomputers also introduced people to programming and multimedia: many future computer graphic artists or musicians cut their teeth on an Amiga or an Atari ST. This period ended for two reasons: the growth of pirated game copies and, above all, the weaknesses inherent to the hybrid character of these machines. They were rapidly found to no longer have the technological and financial weight needed to confront the true game consoles coming from Japan and the true microcomputers: the PCs or Apples. In 1989, the manufacturers of this type of machine stopped production, and most went bankrupt. However, in the land of the rising sun, Nintendo was flourishing as a quasi-monopoly, and in the west, the fortune of Bill Gates had not finished growing.

The fourth cycle corresponds to the triumph of the Japanese company Nintendo, with the Super NES, and the half-Japanese company Sega, with the Megadrive. It is also marked by the development of games for the PC and the appearance of adventure and puzzle games like *Myst* or *Wolfenstein 3D*, as well as role-playing games like *Final Fantasy*. At the end of this period, in 1995, Sega's hero Sonic the Hedgehog seemed to triumph over Mario.

Sonic Heroes (Sega/Sonic Team, 2004).

The fifth cycle corresponds to the appropriation by games of new multimedia technologies, which had not been developed with this goal: treatment of 3D images in real time, parallel computation with dedicated processors, use of CD-ROM as storage support, and games on local networks and the Internet. It also saw the entry of a new actor, Sony, with its PlayStation console. The struggle between Sony and Nintendo raged and swept Sega, who ultimately retired from the console market, to the side. This period saw the birth of the first video-game heroine, Lara Croft, the appearance of games which persist in a graphic universe (*EverQuest*, *Ultima Online*), and multiplayer FPS's like *Doom*, and then *Half-Life*. Nintendo was alone in the market of pocket consoles, and the Pokémons were the representatives of a new child universe. The sales figures of video games surpassed ticket sales in movie theaters. In the euphoria of the new economy, the stock prices of game-publishing companies took flight. In 2001, the speculators, who confused games with the still smoky promises of the Internet, retreated. While, two years previously, people payed top dollar for stock in completely unknown companies, in 2001 the same people acted as if video games didn't exist. This, combined with the announcement of new consoles, provoked an unprecedented crisis in the world of games.

According to Le Diberder, we are thus in the sixth cycle, which has seen the entry of Microsoft into the arena and the bloody struggle between the three consoles: the PS2, the GameCube, and the Xbox. The rest of this book therefore deals with this state in the world of games. All the same, we will not place ourselves strictly within the confines of this universe, which we expect will explode and swarm out into the greater collective world of media.

The Process of Video-Game Production

Economy of the Game Market

In terms of the market, the overall world of video games carries itself very well. With sales figures on the order of 23 billion dollars in 2005 (PC and mobile games), revenues of 5 million dollars for online games, and growth between 10% and 12%, it is in an enviable position. It may be considered as the third media market, behind television, CD-ROM, and DVD, and on the same level as ticket sales in the film industry. Of course, the history of games is marked by depressions, which generally precede striking technological leaps (each generation of consoles) and some gloomy minds predict such a crisis in 2007. But such prognostications are hazardous to make, in this era of growth for various network games. In terms of sales, a certain optimism seems to us to be well-merited. On the other hand, video-game companies are going through a grave structural crisis, which results from changes in production processes and, closely related to this, distribution, via mobile phones and the Internet.

The complexity inherent in video-game creation induces an evolution in production processes and professions: each component of a game is a project in its own right, which demands specific abilities on the part of professionals in the relevant field. Overall, writing and integration of the various components is an aspect of this process which, while mirroring the cinematic process, has specific features connected to its gaming and interactive characteristics.

This evolution in techniques and content has completely transformed the production of games. The growing complexity of content and of the production process results in considerable growth in development costs and in the associated risks. Just a few years ago, some game production enterprises would handle of all necessary activities for the creation and even the distribution of their products. They developed the necessary tools for the creation of a game, produced and edited its contents, and performed their own marketing. That era is gone. The field of video games is now divided into various sectors, and its modes of production and distribution are diversified. The present industry crisis is a consequence of this transformation, which should ultimately lead the gaming industry to maturity, as well as leading to the recognition of its innovative form of expression, capable of producing as many masterpieces as it does flops.

The principal movers in the sector, directly connected to the processes of creation and production, are the publisher, the development studio, and the distribution chain. In addition, video games are tied to specific technology. This in turn involves the PC industry (sound and graphics cards, dedicated peripherals, etc.) and, above all, the console makers, who play a dominant role in the video-game market. Finally, recent years have seen the appearance of an industry that produces software designed specifically for video games: graphics engines, audio, artificial intelligence, physical simulations, network game platforms, and software for managing the elements of a project in development (configuration management). The interrelations between the players in the gaming world, those of telecommunications, and those of media are beginning to be established. They are tied to the development of game distribution (or of associated services) through the detour of the networks, as well as to the utilization of content and franchises on different audiovisual supports.

The video-game market can be globally divided between:

- the products for personal computers (PCs), which are intended for use by individuals or a closed group of players;

- the products for consoles such as the Sony PS2, the Microsoft Xbox, and the Nintendo GameCube. From a technical point of view, all of these technologies now have network capabilities with the result that consoles should have almost the same market as PC games. This is however not entirely the case. For example, women and players older than 20 are more likely to play games on a PC than on consoles.

- the products for "portable" consoles; most of which are found at this time on Nintendo products such as Game Boy and Nintendo DS. However, this type of game already exists for personal digital assistants (PDA's) and on the new generation of mobile phones. The Nokia N-Gage, a machine born from the monstrous coupling of a telephone and a Sega console, is an example of this area of development. The Nintendo DS and the Sony PSP are two powerful new portable consoles with different target markets. Nintendo capitalizes on the 5–12-year-old market and also attracts older players who like to play short games, for example, while traveling or commuting. Sony offers mobile games with the same functionality as PS2 console games: gaming and the ability to play movies and music at high quality. Some games for portable telephone are distributed, it would seem, with more than 250 million copies;

- the massively multiplayer games, which are basically marketed in the form of a monthly subscription. Such a subscription is normally priced at around 15 dollars per month (Lejade, 2002).

Out of the pre-tax price of a console game, 35% goes to large-scale distribution, 51% to the publisher, and 14% to the development studio. The publisher repays around 22% of the selling price to the console manufacturer. The average price of a recent game of this type is 50 dollars (Le Diberder, 2002).

According to F. Fries (Fries, 2003), the typical budget for a console video game, aiming for sales of more than one million units, is the following (in millions of dollars):

Development	$6 M	16.7% (sub-contracted to the studio)
Marketing	$6 M	16.7%
Manufacturing	$12 M	33.3% (paid to console manufacturer)
Marketing/licenses	$2.5 M	6.9%
Distribution	$7 M	19.5%
Margin (before taxes)	$2.5 M	19.5%
Total	$36 M	100%

The minimum development cost of a game (for example, for mobile-phone games) is at least $360,000. There are games which have cost nearly $24 million dollars for big productions, and next-generation games may exceed these numbers substantially. Games made only for local markets, except the U.S. and Japan, are therefore not financially viable, since the point at which sales will break even is at a minimum of 100,000 units sold (for console and PC games).

The Players

The game publisher has a role comparable to a film producer. It provides the basic financing for development, for promotion of the product, for its manufacture, and for large-scale distribution. Contrary to the case for films, there are few mechanisms for pre-purchase, help in creation, or independent production, (production that does not rely on the financing of publishers). We note, nevertheless, that we have begun to see the appearance of independent producers and the use of subsidies (in Europe) similar to those of film creation for financing the initial phase of game definition (preproduction; see the next section).

The development studio is, properly speaking, the creator of the game. It takes charge of its writing and realization and organizes all of the necessary professional sub-groups. It is selected by a publisher through one of two approaches: either the studio produces a game project at its own expense (preproduction) and then pitches it to different publishers, or it is selected through a bid made to the publisher to produce a game whose theme is imposed (in the case of licenses bought by the publisher). In general, the development studio cedes the entirety of its intellectual property rights to the publisher.

The basic process of distribution takes place in large retailers, like Walmart, Best Buy, COMP USA, etc. In this setting, the profit margin for the retailer of video games is greater than that which comes from other audiovisual products. This is a sign of the still limited weight of games in the economy of leisure publication. Specialized distribution of games in game stores is more common in the U.S. and Japan than in Europe.

The console manufacturers are also dominant players in the sector. The console games, much more protected against piracy than PC games, dominate the market at present. Every console game must be approved by the console manufacturer. This is in turn associated with rather large royalties, which constitute the manufacturer's principal source of revenue. It imposes its own norms of quality, ergonomics, and even of content, which it controls throughout the production process: a game may not be published without the approval of the manufacturer. Moreover, the console manufacturer imposes upon the publisher the subcontractors who will be charged with game manufacture. This dominating influence is all the more perverse in that console manufacturers are themselves game publishers.

The sectorization of the gaming industry has led to a growing separation between the functions of creation and publication. Another consequence, which it seems will continue to grow, is the development of software products designed specifically for this market. Every game relies on generic software that creates the images and sounds in real time, simulates physical laws, supplies behavioral models for the game characters, and so on. Such software is called the "game engine." Its functions are used by the programmers who code the game. Once upon a time, each studio had its own engine. However, present-day engines are very complex collections of software, with multiple functions, requiring very diverse abilities for their development. It is impossible to pay for the development of such software with one game, or even a collection of games. The production of a game thus becomes more and more similar to that of a film, with a high turnover in personnel. A studio, even an important one, therefore has an increasingly difficult time in keeping up with all the necessary knowledge for the maintenance of such software. A studio which produces its own engine becomes analogous to a film producer who makes its own cameras.

Multi-platform game engines (or game middleware), i.e., those able to generate the code game for several consoles or PC"s, are the efficient solution to the domination of consoles manufacturers; a studio is able to make the choice of the first console on which the game will be launched. The software of Criterion (RenderWare), is used in numerous well-known games and, the GTA series, in particular, is considered as the best example of this tool. In 2004, the leading game publisher Electronic Arts (EA) acquired Criterion. There is now a risk that the next generation of Criterion products will be dedicated only to EA games. There are independent challengers like the Unreal engine or the Torque Game Engine from GarageGames, as well as shareware with a set of limited functions, but the game engine for the next console generations will not be available, at least, before 2007.

Production Teams and Processes

The design and production of a game is a long and complex process. It takes four to eight people, working for six to eight months, to create a simple game (for Game Boy or portable telephone) and the production of a major game for PC's or consoles can occupy a team, having between forty and a hundred members at its largest, for three years.

The figure at the top of page 24 gives an idea of team organization, keeping in mind that this structure borrows numerous characteristics from film production, but could vary considerably from one studio to another and according to the importance of projects.

Overall, there are five large classes of professions: the game designers (including both the overall game designers as well as the level designers) who specify the universe of the game, its rules, and its levels and write the dialogue; the graphics artists and animators; the sound designers and musicians; the programmers who develop either the basic mechanisms (the game engine) or the game itself; and finally, the producers.

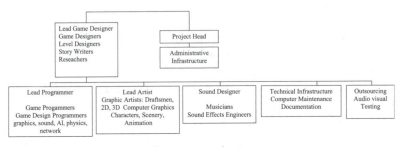

Video-game professions.

The design of a game begins with the composition of a short out-line, equivalent to a film synopsis. It describes the type of game envisaged, the target audience, the target platforms (consoles and PC), and a proposed release date. This outline is submitted to an editorial committee: either within the studio, if it is the originator of the project, or with the publisher, in the other case. If the project is approved, the design phase will last one to three months and will unite a small team of two to eight people. This phase allows for specification of what the game will become, as much from the point of view of writing as of its audiovisual presentation. It also gives an opportunity to show evidence of its originality, as well as to evaluate its technical difficulties, production plans, and cost. A playable model will often be constructed. At the end of this phase, the studio must either find a financial backer or abandon the project. In the case where financing is found (at least partially), the game design is finished, and the different professional groups (graphic artists, sound designers, programmers) create the objects (characters, environments, etc.) which make up the game's universe. Production, properly speaking, may last from two to three years. This allows for the creation of different levels (level design) within the game by positioning the various objects in the game's space, the construction of the puzzles which the player will have to solve, and the determination and subsequent programming of the abilities of the enemies that the player will confront. This process terminates with a testing phase.

Contrary to "classic" computer engineering, which follows a development process in the so-called "V" model (Printz, 2000), in which a piece of software is first specified, then designed, produced, and finally tested at different levels, the production of a game is based on successive improvements performed on a prototype. In fact, it is impossible to measure the quality of a game and the effectiveness of its rules without actually trying it out. A paper analysis, however thorough it may be, will not allow one to detect a weakness of the interface or a bad regulation of rule parameters that causes the game to be too simple or too difficult. Likewise, image and sound quality can only be appreciated through practice. As a result, throughout the production process, a game may be abandoned whenever the publisher feels that it does not have the requisite qualities or no longer relates to the desires of the market.

In particular, the final game-testing phase thus begins with an evaluation of its qualities (alpha testing) and may still lead to abandonment of the game. If it is not abandoned, it passes on to a debugging phase. An army of fanatic teens assaults the game in every nook and cranny, to try to discover its weaknesses. The actions of the players and the history of the game are saved, allowing the bugs to be corrected. It is important to note that console games undergo this treatment twice: once at the development studio and once with the manufacturer, who must approve it before production. The testing for consoles is simpler, since the console configuration is unique, while the various possible configurations one may find for a PC are practically innumerable. Testing for a console game must be of extremely high quality since, up until 2003, it was impossible to download a corrective patch for the game onto the console, via the Internet, and it is still not the practice for security reasons. As a result, console games are much more reliable than PC games.

The Economic Future of Games

The video-game economy is the very image of a field that is trying to find itself. An analysis of present problems within this sector reveals signs of structural immaturity. In this sector, a publisher may regularly abandon projects which have cost it many millions of dollars and automatically provoke the liquidation of a studio. A studio may hire an intern with a crucial level of responsibility, then at the end of three months lay him off because there is nothing more to pay him with. It may take care of a resource as indispensable as the graphic artists with short-term contracts which are continually renewed. Thus, by all evidence, this field is still trying to establish its practices. These examples, witnessed in three years of teaching experience, are drawn from French companies, but they capture (perhaps, in exaggerated form) the problems of the industry.

Let us mention as examples:

- the emerging organization of the various players in the gaming sector induces a relative weakness in commercial and political power compared with more classic sectors like distribution, film, TV, and telecommunications. This translates into a difficulty in assigning value to their rights in the matter of intellectual and artistic property;

- complex and very slow production processes (taking two to three years) compared to product lifetimes (six months) and to the high risk (less than 20% of games which pass the stage of preproduction are completed);

- the absence of independent systems of production, already mentioned.

- The difficulty of clearly defining the status of game creators. Most games (except perhaps those created in Japan) do not have credits, and if there are some, they are well hidden. Without notable exceptions, you will never find on the cover of the game box *The Return of the Ghost* . . . , followed by the name of a creator or a group of creators. If it is the game of someone, it's the game of the publisher or eventually the game of the studio. In this case, the game industry takes the status of software publishers disclaiming the cultural contents of games. Publishers are so anxious to keep all rights that they miss the great marketing advantage of having famous creators. Maybe they could take some lessons from the cinema industry.

The economic landscape of gaming in five or ten years is difficult to predict. It is possible that the entire sector will come under the control of the main players in film, TV, or telecommunications. It is possible that the large publishers and the console manufacturers will profit from the dynamics of the present to impose themselves as major players in the cultural industry. The ambitions of Sony and Microsoft are in this regard significant. For game lovers, this constitutes a beautiful game of Monopoly to be observed.

- 2 -

The Cheater's Novel,
or How to Write a Video Game

Introduction

A video game is not a linear story—the basic experience of the player is the sensation of being an actor within the story and of enjoying great freedom of action. The focus of a game also rests on a collection of mechanisms for creating dramatic tension and resolving conflicts, conventionally used in linear writing, but difficult to implement in an interactive universe in which the author has no control over how the action plays out. Moreover, a game is subject to a strong commercial constraint: the length of time needed to reach the end must be marked out (with the exception of persistent games). Typically, a beginning player must put in at least one hundred hours to finish, and a dedicated and experienced player from ten to fifty hours. The player must therefore be furnished with all the keys for success, while leaving him the sensation that he discovered them on his own. In the film *eXistenZ*, David Cronenberg points out, through the speech of a novice player, that "free will is obviously not a big factor in this [game]." "It's like real life. There's just enough to make it interesting," the game designer philosophically replies.

The creator of a game is therefore trapped within this system of constraints, which has in turn led to the development of a very original method of writing, borrowing from classical linear forms, from the design of social games (board games, card games, etc), and from the principles of interaction developed by computer scientists.

In this chapter, we analyze this process by elaborating on four aspects of game creation: game design, level design, immersion methods, and gameplay.

The writing of a game proceeds schematically in two steps. The first consists in designing the universe, a goal for the game, and some rules. This is called *game design*. The designer outlines the context (epoch, style, historical or mythical references), the geography and principles of navigation within this universe, and the principal characters. The gameplay includes the objective of the game and its principal stages, the type of quests that the player will have to complete, and the gaming mechanisms used (revelation of partial objectives, obstacles, techniques for solution). It is then necessary to develop the perceptive characteristics of the universe, the principles of interface of the game, the training process—everything which relates to the ergonomics of the game. This description is made during the preproduction phase and affects the financing. In consequence, the designer must exhibit the principal innovations of the game, and he must describe all of the objects which make up its universe.

The second step has as its goal the construction of the specific scenarios that take place in this universe. This is called *level design*. The design of such scenarios is based, not on a timeline, but on the positioning of objects in space and on logical rules.

Game Design: Conceiving a Universe

A game is first of all an imaginary universe which may be neither revealed nor created by following the linear track of a story. The first stage in any design is that of imagining and describing all of the *object classes* which exist in this universe.

The notion of object is understood here in the computer-science sense of the term. Something has the status of object because it can produce or experience an action which has an influence on the progress of the game. Consider, for example, a door. If it is possible to open it, it is an object; if it is only an element of the decor, it does not really exist as an object. It will instead be more of an optical illusion painted on the wall (or a texture, in the jargon of computer graphics). A *class* of objects is made up of all the objects which have the same perceptive and active characteristics. The perceptive characteristics are made up of the visual representation of the object and the sounds which are associated with it. The active characteristics are both the actions which may be caused by an object and the actions which have an effect on this object. For example, a dragon can steal, growl, spit fire, and eat the hero. A dragon may also be ridden, wounded, or killed.

Schematically, it is possible to consider three large categories of objects: the constituents of the universe, the ambient objects, and the staging tools. The constituents are the objects that are identifiable as such by the player: the characters, animals, landscapes, buildings, weapons, monsters, and so on. The designer may also create some objects that contribute to the ambiance of the game. For example, if the universe includes both daytime and nighttime settings, a weather system, and varying seasons that affect the lighting and the sounds of the environment, some corresponding classes must be anticipated and their evolution described. Finally, the designer must imagine the objects necessary for staging: the virtual cameras and microphones which will determine the perceptions of the player and the limits imposed on the movement of the player and of the cameras. Numerous games in 3D allow the player to see either from the point of view of his avatar (first-person vision) or from the point of view of a camera generally situated above and slightly behind the avatar (third-person vision). By contrast, it is often necessary to force a camera and a point of view in certain circumstances. This allows for continuity between non-interactive (cinematic) animations and the different levels of the game properly speaking. Fixing a point of view also allows the game to draw the attention of the player to a detail of importance for the stage to come.

Black & White is a strategy game designed by Peter Molyneux, in which the player is a god on a small island. The representation of the god, and therefore the player's avatar, is a hand. It is always seen in the third person. The god is supplied with a good angel and an evil angel, whose advice constitutes one of the sources of help for the player. The characters are of two types: either the inhabitants of the island, classified by sex and profession, or mythical and intelligent creatures who are assistants to the gods. There are also ordinary animals (sheep, pigs, etc.) and plants which serve as sources of food as well as construction materials. The island is furnished with some preexisting decor and buildings. Other buildings are created and destroyed within the context of the game. This game features a day/night chronology and randomized weather. The aim of the game is to have the greatest number of followers, knowing that to do so the player may either behave like a charitable god, loved for his graciousness, or like a demon, feared for his evil deeds. Since the universe is polytheistic, the conquest of souls is the subject of a bitter contest, and wars rage between the gods.

A creature in *Black & White* (Lionhead Studios/Electronic Arts Games, 2002).

A method of writing that involves the definition of all objects before any narration is, in its basic principles, revolutionary. Indeed, although there are many literary or audiovisual works of fiction which exist as a universe before existing as a story (the *Lord of the Rings*, for example), the universe is still revealed to the reader within the framework of a tale. This structure in reading is often just as well a structure for writing: even if the author has imagined from the very beginning the basic constituents of his universe, he fine-tunes the details, to make the ensemble coherent and credible, while constructing the story. This is all the more natural since he explicitly frames the sights and sounds experienced by the reader/spectator. The reader will only know the places and times that the author has chosen, and he will perceive them according to the angle, light, and sight/sound relation determined by the author.

The game designer, even for those games where the player has little freedom, cannot work in this way. In fact, he must deliver the result from this stage of development to the other professional groups, who will then construct the building blocks of the universe: the level designers; the computer graphics designers and the animators for the visual aspect and the principles of animation for characters and environment; the sound designers for the sounds associated with objects and with possible events; and finally the programmers, who will describe in computer language all of the possible actions and behaviors.

The designer is not necessarily the master of how the game unfolds, how the camera moves, etc. The narratives, when they exist, are only developed later by the level designer, who himself leaves the player some latitude in decision making, or at least in movement. An object must therefore be evaluated on the basis of how it may be used by the level designer or perceived by the player in a great number of situations, as well as from a number of different points of view that are not predetermined.

Let us give two simple examples of the impact of this method of creation.

A character in a painting, comic book, or animated film is designed to be seen in a certain way. For example, Mickey Mouse's ears are always seen from the front. On the other hand, the 3D computer graphics designer works like a sculptor. He must design a character who can be viewed from every angle, which considerably complicates the task of selecting the significant graphical elements.

In a film, the sound, in general, and the music, in particular, are tied to the scenario and are often an essential element of the drama (Chion, 2003). In games, there is no obligation whatsoever to connect particular music to an object or a place. This is, however, the most natural way to organize the sounds within a game. Specific acoustics are associated to each room of the environment, and a musical loop is associated to each place. Each time the player enters into the room, the sound effects are

Steps in the graphic design of a character from *Rayman 3* (Ubisoft, 2003).

treated in real time according to the virtual acoustics of the room, and the player often hears the same music.

Let us note that to reintroduce drama into this context is a complex problem from the point of view of writing. Which elements measure the dramatic tension, how does one construct music and, more generally, a story which depend on these elements and maintain coherence? This also entails technical problems. We shall return to this point in the section dealing with immersion.

The difference between the two methods of writing can be brought into focus by considering the interfaces of the assembly tools used in the conventional audiovisual world and in the gaming world.

A video assembly tool, for example, is essentially a picture that allows the positioning of visual and sonic elements along a time line, together with the definition of points of synchronization and of transitions between elements (Julier, 2001). It is a chronological weaving of the elements of composition.

A game assembly tool, such as RenderWare Studio, presents itself as a map and a selection of environments. The tool allows access to a library of objects. The designer chooses and places some objects in the surroundings, for example, a door and a button. These objects may have some non-interactive precalculated behaviors. 3D animation software enables the manufacture of an opening animation and a closing animation for the door while producing, in each case, a sinister sound. It is equally well prepared for a push of the button. The designer has at his disposal a library of programs that define the interactive behavior of the objects. For example, when the player presses the button, the button object emits a message "button pushed," and when the door receives the message "open," it opens. The game designer will thus link up the two messages, which allows one to open the door by pushing the button.

There is no explicit or implicit description of time: the composition produces a spatial and logical relation between objects. We show in the next section how the narrative is organized in space. Computer programmers have a methodology appropriate for this method of writing, called object-oriented design. Some of the artists who produce interactive installations, like sculptors and some architects, follow a method of creation close to this. However, it may be noted that, within the narrative domain, it is a very innovative approach; this is all the more true since this method has been formalized and has given birth to some original compositional tools.

We mention as well the existence of tools with an intermediate position, the most famous of which is the Director software from Macromedia. These tools are used most commonly in the design of CD-ROM's or web sites. The tools, derived from the tools of video editing, retain the organizing principle of a time line in order to show the different elements. However, in this representation, all time intervals are taken relative to the various actions taking place and to the events caused by the spectator. The time is not noted in absolute values but according to a numbering system visualized by the sequence of columns along the time axis. A simple computer language (called a script language) allows for the programming of an interactive scenario. For example, at time n (the nth column of the time line) and according to the behavior of one of the objects, it is possible to associate an instruction: "If the player clicks on the object, then move to time k, else continue to $n + 1$."

Although it may be possible to use RenderWare Studio for programming in the form of a script, and to make a design in the form of interaction between objects using Director, the interfaces of these three

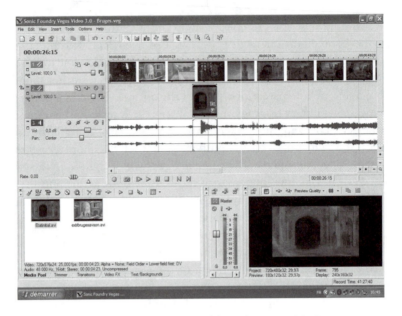

Interface of a video assembly tool (Vegas Video).

tools show us three different visions of writing. In the case of video montage, the structure is purely temporal and at each step, the monitor organizes the total perceptive space of the spectator: it is a linear narration. The natural approach for using Director is to keep a global vision of each scene and to construct a scenario which has many possible sequences according to the actions of the spectator. We shall call such a narrative form a quasi-linear script. With RenderWare Studio, the story is no longer written. What the monitor describes are the relationships between the objects in the universe of the game, with the player's avatar being one of these objects. To introduce a narrative, the level designer uses another approach described in the next section.

Even if a number of adventure games adopt a quasi-linear script structure, the approach through objects is the most original and the most promising. In persistent online games, it is the only possibility. Moreover, it opens the possibility of creating objects whose behavior evolves, and perceptive and narrative forms that automatically generate themselves. These aspects will be taken up again in Chapter 4.

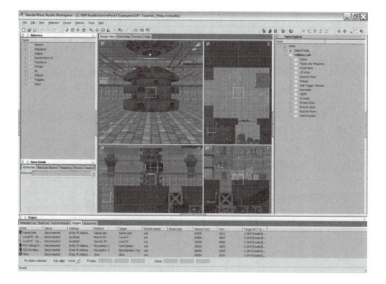

Interface of a game assembly tool (RenderWare Studio).

Level Design: The Technique of the Maze

Design of the successive levels in the game is the second step in the writing process. A level is one of the episodes in the player's interactive adventure, which is unavoidable within the overall structure of the game. It is tied to an objective, either explicit or implicit, which must be accomplished in order to obtain passage to the following level. In single-player games, and in particular in adventure games, this is the element which is plotted out in the most detail. Using the terminology of Guardiola (Guardiola, 2002), a level is made up of a collection of quests. The accomplishment of a quest includes understanding the objective, detecting the obstacles, and finally implementing its solution. The order in which quests are completed is not totally fixed, and a player may be involved in many quests simultaneously. All the same, the logic of the game's rules, the training process that leads the player to complete an increasingly complex series of quests, and, as a consequence, the possibility of creating tension as a narrative mechanism must all work to guide the player to a predictable behavior in space and time. It is nevertheless indispensable that he retains the sensation of freedom.

It is in this phase of the creative process that the idea of the maze comes into play as a writing tool. In general, the designer starts from a representation of the space in which the level unfolds. He then places the collection of objects that are going to define the sequence of quests which will direct the player through completion of the level.

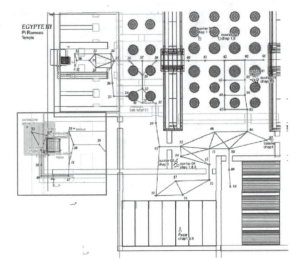

A blueprint used for level design. It indicates the possible paths of the player. *Egypt 3* (Kheops Studio/Dreamcatcher, 2004).

For example, one begins by placing the horrible monster (the Minotaur) that must be defeated at the end of the level (the level's *boss*).

A door is placed to close off an access corridor to the monster. A key is required to go through the door. To kill the monster, one needs a sword and a life potion. The key is hidden in an amphora guarded by two frightful creatures. The philter can only be acquired by paying a large amount of money. To get the money, one must kill other monsters (the Minotaur babies) spread throughout the environment, and so on.

The entry point into the level, as well as the topography and interlinking of quests—whose order is not completely fixed but which is highly constrained by the logic of the puzzles—determine a path through the level that maintains the dramatic tension and terminates in a "happy ending," where the player strikes down the Minotaur and

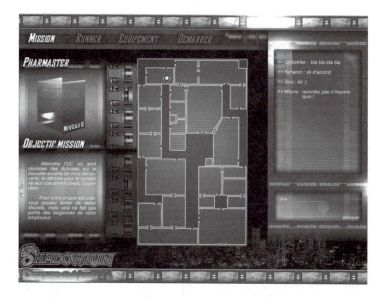

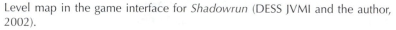

Level map in the game interface for *Shadowrun* (DESS JVMI and the author, 2002).

concludes the level. It is understood that the player does not know the right path(s) beforehand. The search for this (these) path(s), and for the keys to the puzzles that are strewn throughout it (them), is his area of freedom. However, since he must finish the level in a reasonable time, the designer supplies an analogue of Ariadne's thread, which will limit the player's wanderings. The hints may be spoken, textual, visual, or sonic cues which provide details on the quests to be resolved or on the means of procuring useful objects for the remaining part of the game.

This help is often supplied through a map, an indispensable accessory that every hero of a role-playing game keeps in his knapsack.

What is therefore very innovative in this style of writing is the fact that the tale is based on space, not on time, and that the linearization of the story takes into account the player's desire to complete the level and thus to follow the "efficient" route which is suggested to him. We illustrate this with three very different examples.

In the adventure game *Grand Theft Auto* (GTA for the initiates), the player incarnates a small-time thug who must build his career in a town held by different gangs. In each level, he obeys an employer (the Mafia, then the Triads) and finishes the level by eliminating his boss or by changing his colors. Each level is made up of a series of quests (finding the boss's girlfriend, killing a problem-causer, blowing up a building), which is introduced by a short cinematic. To accomplish his mission, the player must steal a car, which allows him to move freely around the city. Most of the missions have no time limit. The player thus has the opportunity to walk around and to accomplish his task at his leisure. In practice, however, he makes use of a dynamic map (like a GPS system), which shows him the shortest path towards the obstacles he is about to confront. This is the path that he follows, in general.

Homeworld is a strategy game that takes place in the future, in outer space. The main focus of the game is on the quality of the real-time, 3D graphics. As in the majority of strategy games, the player must develop an economy and a military structure that will allow him to defeat an enemy race. In *Homeworld 2*, the game is divided into successive battles, each of growing complexity, which entail an adapted sequence of investment choices and combat-unit placements. The space is open-ended, but in the single-player matches, the computer (and, therefore, the game designer) takes the initiative in placing enemy units, which sets up the positioning of the game's various stages. Strategy games are basically laid out as a function of a training process, where the player has great freedom of decision in the organization of resources and units. In the first levels of *Homeworld*, a series of decisions that will aid the defeat of an adversary is strongly suggested by the game's tutorial.

Our final example concerns a game genre that may seem, a priori, to not be the object of any scenario whatsoever: car simulation games. Nevertheless, in the sense of level design, these are the most highly constrained games. Most of these games leave choices for the player concerning his avatar, equipment, the race track, the type of race that he wants to enter, and some options for racing strategy. However, once the level has begun, the player has only to follow the circuit as quickly as possible while avoiding the obstacles.

Immersion Methods

One of the most basic qualities of a game is the sensation of immersion felt by the player, which should impel him to use his controller for many long hours. The definition of immersion leads to many discussions among researchers. We consider immersion (or presence) as the absence of disbelief. Schematically, the sensation of immersion relies on narrative control, game perception, and the playful appeal of the game's rules.

It is possible to combine these three aspects while remaining close to the classical rules of plot construction (Szinlas, 2001), as well as the rules of construction for a board game or a sport. The principle that allows this consists of dynamically adapting the sonic and visual ambiance, as well as the complexity of quests, as a function of the amount of difficulty in a level.

This allows for the development of tensions that approach the climax of a linear scenario. A very simple and often-used example of this principle consists of injecting more and more enemies into a battle that the player is winning and heightening the musical tension as a function of the number of sword strokes, up until the death of the boss. One then passes to a restful cinematic.

Even though this method is quite interesting and merits a good deal of research, in most games immersion relies on other techniques. To understand this, we consider an analysis performed by Claude Bailblé

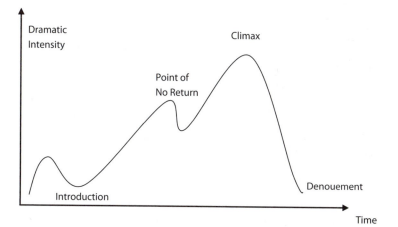

Dramatic structure of a conventional linear scenario (novel, play, musical work).

(Bailblé, 1999). Narrative control is based on principles that have long ago been analyzed in the framework of novels, musical works, and film. The attention of the spectator is maintained through cycles of imposed psychological tension and release. In a cinematic framework, for example, this relies on the possibility of total control over the chronology of the story and on a physical passivity on the part of the spectator, which increases his concentration. This permits a very rapid variation of the psychological tension, which in turn is associated with the stimulation of emotional memories. The spectator does not really "see" a film. Rather, through the film he relives a succession of emotions that he has memorized and which are stimulated by the scenario. In real life, when we are angry, we need a period of at least a few dozen minutes to calm ourselves down and pass on to another emotional climate. While listening to music or watching a film, however, we can pass through a dozen of the most varied emotional states in less than an hour.

A video game does not really enter into this psychological scheme, since the player is a participant in the narrative—through the decisions made, but also through physical action. Even if the graphical and sonic characteristics of a game universe have great evocative power, the development of psychological tension does not follow the rhythms of a story, but rather that of decisions, successes, and failures on the part of the player, just as in "real" life. This is the reason why it is often very boring to watch someone play a game.

In a given level of one of the games from the *Final Fantasy* series (*Final Fantasy X*, for example), the player has control over a repetitive series of battles against diverse creatures. These fights are followed with stages of strategic decision-making, which allow for the optimization of the heroes' abilities as a function of the result of the preceding fight. For a good player, the outcome of each battle is nearly guaranteed at the beginning of the confrontation: if he has played correctly and not wandered too soon into a dangerous zone, he knows that he is going to win. If not, he must flee as quickly as possible. A sequence of this type can last for more than an hour. The ambiance supplied by graphics and sound is always the same. Once a passive spectator has admired the characters and surroundings and listened to the music loop, he can only remain interested in the match if he evaluates the strategy of the player. Despite the audiovisual appearance of the game, the passive spectator is

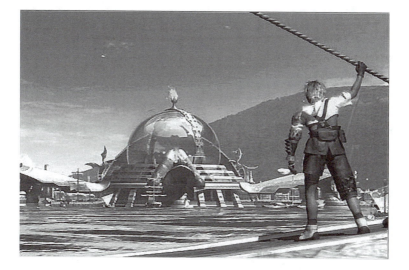

Final Fantasy X (SquareSoft, 2002).

closer in nature to a viewer of a game of chess than to that of a television program.

However, game designers can of course play on the mechanisms of tension that arise in daily life. In the first level of the game *Black & White*, which is implicitly a phase of initiation, the player, who as we recall is a god, travels his island and meets a native, who begs him to perform a miracle: "Lord, find the sheep of my herd, lost on the mountainside." The god, who is often basically good, leaves in quest of the sheep. He finds one, and then two, and while passing through a grove, he falls on another pained soul: "Lord, find my wounded brother, who is lost in the woods," and soon another: "Lord, help me to build my boat."

The god throws himself into more and more quests and begins to experience the same type of stress as an overwhelmed manager. He nearly has need of a Post-It note to list everything he needs to do. A Post-It note, in the form of a magic list, is for that matter available at the temple, listing the number of quests begun and the percentage completed. Here, the game designer uses, not emotional memory, but the memory of everyday stresses in order to immerse the player. A god may not leave his faithful in suffering for very long. This sensation of urgency is heightened through a very accelerated flow of time, each day lasting only a few minutes, with a strong opposition between day and night atmospheres and very short dawns and twilights.

Nevertheless, this mechanism is purely psychological and does not result from the rules of the game. In reality, the player has all the time he wants at his disposal to conclude each quest and can attack them sequentially. The computer contents itself with measuring his level of experience and his abilities in order to decide when to pass to the next level. However, as soon as the player begins to take his time and seems to be thinking that, after all, god has eternity to himself, a small angel or small devil comes to remind him of all the prayers that he has in the oven.

Gameplay: A Gigantic Bluff

Gameplay is the factor in immersion that distinguishes games from traditional narrative forms. The preceding section may lead one to believe that the interest of a game is tied to the subtleness of its rules. In general, this actually accounts for nothing. It is true that a good game is usually "a series of interesting decisions," but here we are talking about the interest of the player in a single duel against the machine—a player rarely replays a single-player adventure game that he has completely finished. This distinguishes single-player video games from card games or board games, and makes them more like books, or video or DVD rentals.

In this section, we only consider single-player games, in which the player confronts the machine. Gameplay includes both the short-term goals and the more long-term objectives that are assigned to the player. These goals and objectives are ranked by level of difficulty. One must define the nature of the obstacles and the choices that will allow one to circumvent these obstacles while distinguishing, according to the objectives, the strategic and tactical choices. At the same time, one must fix the rules for the player and the rules for the machine. Finally, an essential element of the gameplay is the manner in which it will be revealed to the player.

There are some simple principles that any good gameplay must respect, which are developed in treatments of video-game design (Rollings, 2003):

- A choice should be interesting and therefore should have both positive and negative aspects. A real choice leaves a sensation of regret, like choices in life. Thus a good game will not allow a strategy that either always loses or always wins. One must therefore use intransitive choices similar to the game Rock, Paper, Scissors: a choice wins one time out of two and loses one time out of two. Some choices A, B, and C are *intransitive* if the fact that A is preferable to B, and B to C, does not necessarily imply that A is preferable to C. One must introduce short-, medium-, and long-term consequences to every decision. For example, the number of objects that the avatar can use is limited: taking a cannon rather than a pistol could be inconvenient in the situations where one needs to run. This little scrap of paper seems quite useless, but is perhaps the key to future riddles ...

- A rule should be fair: the player should be able to anticipate and circumvent an obstacle. If he fails, it is his own fault. In the first version of *Prince of Persia*, the player has to take a passage which contains a trap. Because of the camera's initial position, the player cannot see the trap and finds himself caught on the first attempt. This type of rule should be forbidden. One must not forget that the all-knowing computer, at once both player and judge, can very easily win—it suffices for it to announce "game over."

- In fact, the player must win. Because of this, it is necessary to progressively supply him with the requisite help needed to get past the obstacles without losing interest in the game.

These different points are nothing but the manifestations of a much more general principle. The rules of a game are usually quite simple; what accounts for its apparent complexity and interest is that the rules are not known to the player. The manual, which is rarely consulted, carries only a very schematic description of the universe. The player throws himself into the adventure and discovers enemies, traps, and strategies in a smoothly controlled learning process that gives him a sensation of accomplishment, which is essential for maintaining interest in the game. He becomes stronger, gains greater understanding of the hostile universe that surrounds him, and defeats increasingly larger monsters and more complex puzzles. He asserts himself as the hero of the game. Nevertheless, all of this is nothing but a gigantic bluff. The game designer has hidden the rules and dynamically modifies them as a function of the player's progress and, in some cases, of his effectiveness. If he loses too often, he is furnished with some assistance to help him extricate himself. When he fights all monsters with one kick and two magic spells, the game sends him monsters who are resistant to this strategy. He will have to find a new combination of attacks (a new *combo*) to win. He will emerge greater in the game and in his own esteem.

To be convinced that gameplay is based on this principle, and that all quest and level construction follows a simple, although unknown, logic, it suffices to read one of the *game guides*, which describe solutions for a game. These are not rules or strategies, but rather directions: begin by picking up the axe, don't forget the health potion, kill the three bugs on the right, pass the isle of no return, etc. These manuals reveal only one of the possible linear narratives that have been imagined by the game designers.

By revisiting the classification given in Chapter 1, this analysis of gameplay can be formalized. It is usual to distinguish the games based on a collection of rules, also called games of emergence, (Juul, 2005), whose interest resides in the complexity of possible rule combinations, and games based on a story, or games of progression, in which obstacles (puzzles, action sequences) are presented successively. The interest of challenges in games come from the fact that they are not predictable, and the game evolution surprises the player. In games of emergence, this surprising effect comes from the fact that the player is unable to plan all possible outcomes of the game. In games of progression, the player is surprised because he doe not know the rules. In order to distinguish a game of emergence from a game of progression, Juul suggests consulting the game guide. If the game guide is presented in the form of general rules, such as "to defeat demons with three tails, hit two times on the head and one time on one of the tails," it is a game of emergence. If the game guide is presented in the form of contextual directions, such

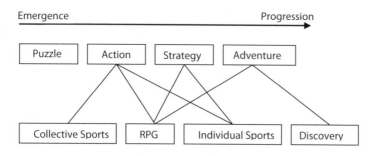

Games of emergence and games of progression.

as "upon entering the second room of the castle, avoid the three-tailed demons and move through the door on the left," it is a game of progression. However, the game guide is in fact a reconstitution of the gameplay, as it was imagined by the game designer.

Even though this distinction seems fundamental to us with respect to the notion of gameplay, and therefore should be of interest for the game, this is highly debatable. The "most" emergent games are the puzzle games. An original video game which is not a puzzle game is not comparable to chess, or even to solitaire games. There are many reasons for this. The fact that a game is rarely replayed has already been mentioned. Likewise, the design of a game like chess took many hundreds of years, and the amazing achievements of computers in the role of chess players were the result of forty years of research. By contrast, the time taken to create a video game is around two to three years, and its life time relatively brief, often less than one year. Gameplay that is too complex, using artificial intelligence that is just a little too elaborate, cannot be tested sufficiently during game production and may lead to problems during play.

By all definitions, strategy games should be games of emergence. This is not always the case. The complexity of the player's strategies is connected to his ignorance of the rules of the game and not to their complexity. It can be interesting in this regard to consult the game guide of a strategy game like *Homeworld 2*, or of an RPG like *Final Fantasy X*.

In practice, original games of emergence are action games. Indeed, these games are based on a training of reflexes, which implies that the rules and mechanisms vary little during the progress of the game.

A good criterion to distinguish a game of progression from a game of emersion is its ability to be played in multiplayer competitive mode with the computer replaced by a human player. In this case, the rules must be known to all of the players. All of the big fighting and FPS games satisfy this criterion. Some strategy games, like *Starcraft*, are symmetric games that are played on networks, whose rules are completely known. The better players of these games often prefer playing on networks to playing with the computer.

Another criterion for judging the emergent character of a game is whether or not its outcome or duration is known. Many commercial games give a definite answer for this criterion (the game length), which is evaluated by the specialized press. On the other hand, some strategy and action games can be replayed without any real time limit, either because the goal of the game is not fixed or because it presents itself as a series of matches which has no overall outcome. For example, *SimCity* involves a strategy of urban planning that has no fixed goal. What does it mean to be a good mayor? Each player can give his own interpretation to this goal. Likewise, it is possible to indefinitely confront the computer in the combat rounds of a game like *Tekken*, as long as the player does not become bored and does not know how to beat the computer with every punch. Games with fixed goals and lengths certainly have a more progressive and less emergent character than the others. Note that multiplayer persistent games are played on the Internet without any limit on game length and without any explicit goal. In this case, the two preceding criteria are combined.

Recent research in artificial intelligence (Spronck, 2003) confirms our analysis of the simplicity of gameplay. Peter Spronck has developed a fairly simple training system, which uses a collection of game rules that a player may use to construct a strategy and win in any given situation (a quest in Guardiola's sense of the word). By replaying the same situation a certain number of times, leading either to success or failure, the system classifies the rules as a function of their effectiveness. Spronck uses primarily the best-ranked rules, but with a probabilistic strategy. Used in the framework of a recent RPG, *Neverwinter Nights*, the training system takes the place of the player and confronts the strategy of the computer in single-player mode (the AI of the game).

At the end of about thirty matches, the training system beats the computer practically every time. On the other hand, any slightly battle-

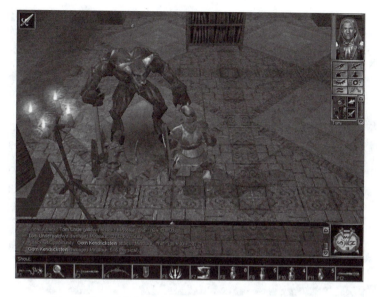

Neverwinter Nights (BioWare Corp, Infogrames, 2002).

hardened player will learn the same thing much more rapidly. From this we may draw the following conclusions: the gameplay strategy of *Neverwinter Nights* is rudimentary; it retains its interest because the player is only supposed to be confronted with any given situation a limited number of times (fewer than thirty). He then passes on to another situation which requires more training.

A study completed by Jesper Juul (Juul, 2004) allows us to explicitly state one principle of immersion connected to gameplay: "At every instant within a game, a player has created for himself a collection of methods and strategic rules which he has devised and which he applies (the player's repertoire). One strength of a good game is the ability to constantly challenge the player, which in turn leads him to constantly find new strategies, apart from those already in his repertoire. A bad game is one in which either the player is incapable of refining his repertoire, or he makes use of a dominant strategy (which wins every challenge) and, because of this, has no need to improve his repertoire." This analysis is illustrated by a video game of the puzzle type, *ChuChu Rocket!*

ChuChu Rocket! (Sega/Sonic Team, 2000).

The objective is to lead mice through a labyrinth while being chased by cats. The levels are distinguished by the nature of the labyrinths. In the first levels, the player develops strategies for avoiding cats according to the principles of billiards. In the following level, this approach no longer works, and the player must discover how to control the movement of the cats.

Beyond Juul's conclusions, this example shows that even for this game, an essentially emergent game, the complexity comes from the evolution of the rules from one level to the next and the incomplete information that the player has at his disposal.

Our analysis leads us therefore to believe that the great majority of single-player games have very simple, hidden gameplay. This assumption has a number of different exceptions, which become more and more numerous with the development of new types of games and growth in the maturity of others. Some strategy games, like *SimCity*, have seen numerous versions. The most recent are the result of a technical process of gameplay improvement that extends over more than twenty years. The gameplay thus becomes truly complex. Finally, the multiplayer games have different principles. For example, when they are played in groups on a local network, like *Counter-Strike*, these games are the objects of discussions concerning the rules and strategies on a world-wide level. They resemble a codified team sport. Finally, persistent online games, treated in the following chapter, raise a completely different set of issues.

Conclusion: What Makes Video-Game Design Different

This chapter has introduced some ideas about the design of single-player games; in the next chapter, we will look at the relationship between multiplayer games and media. In both cases, the originality of games is to place the player as the kernel of the design process. Of course, books or films are often written for a dedicated public; an artist working on an interactive installation may take into account the reception of his piece, but the game designer must have the player's behavior and satisfaction in mind.

This begins at the early stage of the design process when the type of player is chosen: male hardcore gamers between 12 and 20, 30-year-old casual gamers playing on their mobile phones in the subway, etc. But this is a standard marketing approach. The whole gameplay design is based on a psychological and sociological model of the player. Jasper Juul's analysis shows the use of the psychological process of will power; Guardiola (Guardiola, 2000) uses in his game design courses the notion of gameplay loop, the goal of which is to drive the player into a controlled sequence of tensions. The definition of meaningful play given by Salem and Zimmerman (Salem, 2005) highlights the player's relationship with the game system:

> Meaningful play in a game emerges from the relationship
> between player action and system outcome; it is the process
> by which a player takes action within the designed system
> of a game and the system responds to the action. The
> meaning of an action in a game resides in the relationship
> between action and outcome.

The ability to use games as therapeutic tools (Griffiths, 2005), (Stora, 2005) and, conversely, the possible addictive effects of computer games also shows the important relationship between game design and player psychology. Almost all games include a model of the player. This model may be implicit, but generally you can find it in the game-design documentation. The design of a quest, challenge, or puzzle in a single-player game always involve wondering about the following questions.

- What is the intrinsic interest of the problem in terms of fun?

- How is the player motivated to solve the problem?

- How is the problem presented? Does the player have enough information to solve it?

- At this point in the game and taking into account the profile of the targeted gamer, is the player able to solve the problem?

- Is the problem sufficiently difficult to be interesting?

- Can the resolution process be perceived as a demonstration of clever and interesting decisions (intelligence, skills, etc.)

In multiplayer games, the same questions arise, but their social implications must also be considered.

> A game system is an underlying basic way the game works, as opposed to the content of the game .... Once a game system is in place, the particular–the content–can be changed and manipulated fairly easily. The underlying game system is difficult to change later, as it is an integral part of the game's foundation. At their simplest level, social game systems are those games that support, enable, encourage, reward or punish different social behavior. (Pizer, 2005).

This analysis has to be done repeatedly at all levels of the game. For example, at the higher level, the main questions in an adventure game are the following:

- Is there a story?

- If there is a story, is it anecdotal or is it one of the main motivations of the global player progression?

- If the story is fundamental, how do you construct the narrative to build tension? How does this construction rely on level-design mechanisms (topology, logic of quest, learning process, etc.)?

The designer always has to make some hypothesis about the player. An incoherent model of the player, due to false psychological and social assumptions, may be a major cause of the failure of a game. An example is the relative commercial failure of *The Sims Online*. *The Sims* is probably the most popular game in the world. It is a kind of "God game," as the player has control over the population of a small town. Based on the same universe, the same publisher (EA/Maxis) launched an online game *The Sims Online*. But in online games (see next chapter) the players are involved in real social relationships through their avatars. Even if both games are based on the same perceptive universe, their goals are quite different and motivate separate categories of players.

In the near future, the model of the player will be explicitly coded in the game program. It will be an adaptive model that will learn from the

September 12 is a game about politics and communication (Newsgaming/Powerful Robot Games).

behavior of the player(s). The simplest application is to select different situations and quests to avoid the feeling of repetition. More complex models will try to transform the game according the player's interests. Research in game design can become the foundation of new knowledge at the junction of cognitive science, sociology, game theory, narrative theory, and artificial intelligence. It can be applied to many fields, from online education to political propaganda.

- 3 -

Online Games or
the Return of the War of the Worlds

Introduction

In the eighties, on the Internet as it existed, there were some games known that allowed one to move about textually in a fantasy medieval world. At the beginning of the nineties, these games became multi-user and are known as MUD's: *multi-user dungeons*. The player made use of a terminal with a line connected to a distant computer. The game took the form of questions and answers. At each step, the player received some text of the sort:

"You enter into a dark room. There are two doors: one to the right and one in front of you. There is a table placed in the center of the room with a full glass upon it."

The player responded by typing in a statement such as:

"I open the door in front of me."

or:

"I take the glass and drink what's inside."

In many cases, the game would not understand the player's input. The player had to then find another way to phrase it. However, the text that received no response was stored in a database. Another player could read it and provide a response, which augmented the physical and semantic "size" of the game. It is estimated that when this game was abandoned, it would take more than two years of full-time work to visit the entire universe of the game.

The massively multiplayer online games (MMOG's), also called *persistent games*, appeared at the end of the nineties. The precursors are *EverQuest*, *Asheron's Call*, and *Ultima Online*, released in 1997. More recent are *The Sims*, *Star Wars Online*, and *Final Fantasy* XI. The game which has the greatest number of subscribers is certainly *Lineage*, a Korean game, which claims more than four million permanent players and two million episodic players. *World of Warcraft*, launched in 2004, already has more than five million users spread all over the world. These are the descendants of the MUD's, and they retain the same type of imagination, the persistent character of the universe, and the possibility of intervention by the players themselves. They are also the descendants of virtual communities and Internet chat rooms, and have the same social character. They are reliant on the most recent technological developments, offering a graphic interface with an immense universe organized both by powerful centralized servers and the capacities of game PC's.

MMOG's constitute a radical development in the notion of video games that places them in the field of broadcast interactive media. Online games are published on the Internet, while single-player games use offline electronics publishers. This type of implementation immediately confronts the cultural and economic issues of this new medium.

Network games and their future descendants, the proactive games, open wide the Pandora's box of virtual worlds and communities. They are somewhat frightening because they provide the possibility of a collective electronic drug, of which television was only the precursor. Finally, the MMOG's open up a fascinating field for creativity and experimentation. To construct an MMOG is to resolve all of the problems that are constantly posed to sociologists and economists. How does one create and maintain, in its entirety, a society accepted by all of its members? It also, in a certain sense, realizes the dream of the great mad Architect from *The Matrix*, or of the best of the dictators: to create a happy world at his heel.

We begin this chapter by introducing the MMOG's. As we have already emphasized, the design and realization of persistent network games pose scientific and technological challenges that are both fascinating and important to understand in this creative domain. However, they are also essential in numerous other areas of computer and communication science and technology. We will then go on to address proactive and ubiquitous games. These games change the relationship between the player and the virtual universe, since they intervene in the active life of the player at any time and any place.

Massively Multiplayer Games

Spend Every Evening in the Land of the Lord of the Rings

In practice, most current persistent games are role-playing games—one thus speaks of MMORPG's: *massively multiplayer online role-playing games*. Let us describe the basic idea behind an MMORPG. A new player begins by subscribing to the game and installing it on his computer. He finds himself in a universe, in general of the heroic fantasy type (dungeons, dragons, wizards, and knights, etc.) or of the science fiction type in the *Star Wars* vein. He must construct his avatar and has the choice between several races and, often, two sexes. For example, humans, elves, orcs, and so on, since Tolkien has a large influence on this domain. He must then choose his profession: warrior, craftsman, peasant, magician, etc. He dons the costume of his avatar and leaves in search of companions, since he cannot do very much alone. He often joins an organized group (usually called a guild) and participates in the life of this guild. Depending on his virtual profession, he will be in charge of various activities, from craftwork to hunting or war. He may aim for three varieties of non-exclusive objectives: participating in the social life of the group; starting relationships or friendships; or improving the abilities and wealth of his avatar in order to acquire an elevated social status within the game. This demonstrates that a persistent game does not fix precise goals for the player and does not have a fixed notion of game length in the usual sense of this term. In order for a player to become attached to a game, a certain number of conditions must be met. The game must define an original mythological and historical context, and it must give to the players and groups great freedom of action, as much on the material plane as on the social one. The rules of the game must be sufficiently coherent so that a virtual society may be developed. The virtual universe must be sufficiently large and varied so as to allow repeated emotionally touching experiences and to avoid a sense of boredom. Indeed, an occasional player of persistent games plays a few hours per week, while a devoted player may play a few hours per day.

This allows us to characterize present-day MMOG's. They are immense and persistent universes in constant evolution (universe, social rules, gameplay, AI, etc.). The life-time of the universe and of the player's specific match is not limited. The player enters and leaves the game when he wants to. These are first and foremost social and economic systems in which the ability to improve the powers and social standing of the player's avatar is an essential element of the game. Plot, objectives, quests, and levels are all anecdotal. The sensation of freedom given by the social relationships is primordial. As a consequence, the discovery of unanticipated uses for objects is expected and even encouraged.

EverQuest (Sony Online Entertainment/Ubisoft, 2004).

As both economic and social systems, MMOG's engender all of the behaviors observable in the real world. Violence is a common practice, war one of the game's drivers. Theft and pillaging are often in good form (a prerogative of heroic fantasy), but virtual rape is not yet practiced, to our knowledge. Having said this, the persistence of such a system requires rules—those supplied by the game server, but also those imposed by the leaders of a guild. And, of course, a great variety of associated behaviors is observed. These range from the non-observance of customs of the game's universe to the use of computer pirating technology. We will analyze this aspect in the next section.

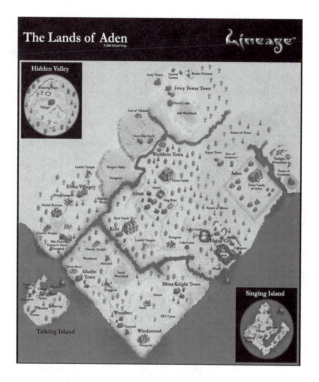

Lineage II (NCsoft, 2004).

Therefore, even without justice, one needs police. These come in three varieties. The first is the control exercised by the players themselves, with most guilds constructed from a charter containing rules of exclusion. There are also rudimentary programmed mechanisms that can control simple behaviors in a chatroom. This technique has existed on the Internet for a long time and has developed hand-in-hand with cybersociety. Finally, MMOG's help to decrease unemployment levels since the game administrators have to hire personnel charged with keeping surveillance on what happens in the virtual universe and, among other things, keeping track of bandits.

The Relationship between Real and Virtual Worlds

Analysis of MMOG's leads to significant examples of the increasing relationship between the virtual world (the game state and its evolution) and the real world, and it foresees the evolution of a cybersociety. Of course, the virtual world is altered by player actions, but sometime the real world can be significantly altered by objects and actions in the virtual world. In MMOG's, this was not initially intended by the game publishers. Proactive and ubiquitous games, presented in the next section, implement this kind of interaction as a design feature.

The first kind of interaction is related to the influence of the virtual economy on the real one. A player modifies and often builds virtual objects. These objects have a value in the game and can be evaluated in virtual currencies. But they also have a value in the real world, for they represent hours and hours of gaming time.

Many virtual characters and items acquired in the virtual world of online games can be traded in the real world. The virtual values of items (e.g., weapons, magic potions, etc.), can result in actual financial transactions. A search on eBay for lineage revealed 357 items for sale relating to *Lineage Online* with starting bids ranging from $5 to $700.

The exchange and the market of virtual goods are also practiced in offline games, like *The Sims*. It is probably the most popular game in the world (48 million players in 2004). For the few readers who do not know this game, we recall that the goal is to manage and give life to a virtual population (the Sims), living in a typical small town. One of the main interests of *The Sims* is the ability to build and exchange virtual objects, like furniture, clothes, etc. These objects can, of course, be exchanged or sold through countless web sites.

Until 2004, this kind of trade was always forbidden in MMOG provider contracts (an example from a contract is given later in this section), but it seems that, as they are not really able to control this

A scene from *The Sims 2* (Electronic Arts/Maxis, 2004).

situation, some publishers are revising their position on this. One of the main problems raised is the nature of intellectual property in interactive virtual worlds. But underneath this subject more complex paradoxes in the relationship between virtual worlds and the real one appear. A fascinating example is given in (Koster 03). Raph Koster analyzed the economy of the MMORPG *Star Wars*. In this economic system, as in most MMOG's, there is no central bank. Virtual money (credits) is created and destroyed dynamically according to player operations. But, as in real life, to be effective the system must maintain a constant mean level of currencies. The analysis of *Star Wars* shows that the amount of money destroyed is much higher than the amount of money created. According to macroeconomics, this should lead to a deflation. As this situation did not appear, Raph Koster investigated:

> A while back we noticed that the game was running at a deficit, and yet there were none of the major effects we'd expect, such as currency becoming incredibly hard to come by, people going bankrupt, etc. Our conclusion was that a lot of the currency out there must have been "counterfeit"— in other words, we had a dupe bug. We promptly started hunting for it, and in fact we not only found it, but were able to mass ban a large number of folks who were clearly involved. . . .

Let's complete this analysis by considering the following fact. All the main virtual currencies can be bought with real dollars on the Internet: being rich in a virtual world allows you, like in the real world, to be an important person. Then, to make some real money, you can forge currencies in virtual worlds and send them into the real one. It is much easier than forging real dollars and much less risky. In the first case, you can be sued by the game provider since you broke the contract; in the second case you may have some big problems with the FBI.

A second example of how games forecast the evolution of society is the analysis of hacking. The following presentation is taken from (Natkin, 2005).

Game hackers are players. As a consequence, they are particularly inventive and clever. Goals of game attacks are much more sophisticated than classical hacking over the Internet: in games, cheaters try to alter subtle rules of the games, time behavior, and ownership rights of virtual objects. A game attacker may have numerous motivations.

- Become a famous hacker.

- Deny the provider service (sabotage against the provider).

- Play without paying.

- Steal the resources of the provider.

- Steal the resources of other players.

- Cheat to win game quests.

- Cheat to acquire virtual resources, which can eventually be sold in the real world.

This list is not exhaustive and can not be the basis of a rigorous classification. From an observable point of view, the goal of an attack can be considered as sabotage (denial of service), theft or cheating to win in the game, but this is a very rough classification.

All classical security definitions rely on the definition of rights and a security policy (Natkin, 2000). An attack is an attempt to perform unauthorized actions according to the security policy. A difficult problem in online games is to characterize the operations that are allowed and forbidden. We consider three levels of rules that can be violated.

Cheating the provider. The relationship between the player as customer and the game provider is generally defined by an explicit contract. For example, in *World of Warcraft*, the player is not allowed to sell virtual objects.

> Note that Blizzard Entertainment either owns, or has exclusively licensed, all of the content which appears in World of Warcraft. Therefore, no one has the right to "sell" Blizzard Entertainments content, except Blizzard Entertainment! So Blizzard Entertainment does not recognize any property claims outside of World of Warcraft or the purported sale, gift or trade in the "real world" of anything related to World of Warcraft. Accordingly, you may not sell items for "real" money or exchange items outside of World of Warcraft.
>
> —An excerpt from the *World of Warcraft* contract
> (Blizzard, 2004).

Cheating other players. This is an attempt to violate the game rules, which must be followed to ensure the fairness of the game. These rules are not always precisely defined. The following presents the rules related to duels in World of Warcraft.

> To start a duel, select the player you wish to duel. Right-click on the player's portrait and select "duel."
>
> - You can't duel in certain areas.
> - You can't duel players you can attack normally.
> - Skills will not increase from use while duelling or engaged in PvP.
> - Dueling players can cast helpful spells on their allies (but not vice versa).
> - Players can no longer swap inventory gear while dueling.

- Dueling is allowed within Everlook.
  —Gameplay rules of a duel (Blizzard, 2004)

Cheating virtual society.   Persistent worlds are regulated by moral rules that allow the virtual social community of the game to be rather stable. These rules may vary from group to group. For example, a member of the Golden Guild (a cooperative group of players) in the game *Dark Age of Camelot* must adhere to the following rules: he must obey the orders of guild hierarchy, he must always help other members of the guild, and he must chat with other members of the guild. In *World of Warcraft*, the chat rules cover the following items.

Highly Inappropriate

- Racial/Ethnic
- Extreme Sexuality/Violence
- Real-Life Threats
- Distribution of Real-Life Personal Information
- Sexual Orientation
- Posting Cheats, Hacks, Trojan Horses, or Malicious Programs
- Impersonating a Blizzard Employee
- Posting Unreleased Content

Moderately Inappropriate

- Harassing or Defamatory
- Major Religions or Religious Figures
- National
- Illegal Drugs or Activities
- Spamming and Trolling
- Advertising
- Discussing Disciplinary Actions
  —Chat rules in MMORPG (Blizzard, 2004)

At the boundary of this category there are "unfair" behaviors. An attack on a novice by an expert player is generally considered unfair.

An attack may combine several actions, each one of which can be considered as a violation of one of the previous classes of rules. For example, an attacker may modify the software of the game, an action that is forbidden according to the provider contract, to gain an advantage over other players.

To show the complexity of the online-game security problem, we present some significant examples.

Numerous MMOG contracts stipulate that a player is not allowed to play without being physically present at the client side. In other words, he must not delegate his role to an autonomous agent or any kind of programmed automaton. This rule is intended to protect servers from overloads: if all the players who have a subscription are always connected, even if they are not physically using the client computer, a MMORPG with 3 million customers will go out of business. This type of attack can be rather easily implemented and is very difficult to detect. Even if it is detected, it is practically impossible to prove that the player is not physically present.

Objects sold and distributed in games like *The Sims* can be passive objects, like 3D furniture, but can also be active objects implemented, for example, as Java applets. The interaction of such objects with the virtual world is supposed to be constrained, as they must not disturb the gameplay. (Poulsen, 2005) reports that a sexy hacked coffee machine was distributed to the community of *The Sims*:

> What nobody had realized was that hacked objects or behaviours would be transferred with the house, and would supersede the game's original functionality for anyone who installed it. So if you download a house with a magic espresso machine in the kitchen, all of your espresso machines in all of your Sims houses and neighbourhoods will become magic. If the house came from a game that has the "No Jealousy" patch installed, your game will henceforth be free of the green-eyed monster as well.

We have not been able to verify this funny hack, but its implementation is quite realistic, and this kind of attack is relevant to the new generation of online games where players are allowed to create active objects.

A cheater can gain an advantage by denying service to other players. A cheater can delay the responses from one opponent in a real-time game by flooding his network connection. This technique can be used for several purposes. First, it allows the cheater to get dangerous opponents out of the game. Other players or the game manager will believe that there is something wrong with the network connection of the victim and agree to kick him out. A more subtle use of this attack is just to slow down the response time of the opponent, which gives great advantages to the cheater.

If you translate the previous examples on possible attacks to the next generation of online cooperative systems like distributed universities, cooperative work systems, online auctions, online voting, etc,, you understand why game hackers are a good subject for analysis, even if you are not really interested in video games.

The relationship between real and virtual worlds must also be considered from psychological and social viewpoints.

The following example shows the reality of the interactions between Korean adolescents and their avatars. The avatars are ever-present in relations between young people, whether it is through their mobile phones, in the chat-rooms, or in online games. Some of these social universes are at the borderline between chatrooms and online games. In these games, teens meet each other through their substitute avatars. The avatars therefore play an essential social role. Therefore, they must be dressed fashionably, their hair properly done, etc. When teens want to change their look, they submit their avatar to an operation of aesthetic surgery. Of course, all of these operations come at a price and according to (Sook-Jin, 2004), a Korean adolescent can spend up to 250 dollars per month dressing his avatar.

The social impact of persistent games spills broadly out of the virtual world. For example, a powerful avatar—that is to say, one having a great number of experience points and a high level in the hierarchy of the game—is precious. It can be sold on the Internet, and not in virtual sols but in cold hard cash. In Korea, some gifted players make a living from this activity, by making their avatars progress very rapidly through the game and then selling them and beginning again with a new avatar.

A clothing supply interface for avatars.

This raises, outside of the evident social problems, legal problems concerned with the ownership of the objects thus constructed. Finally, the "great players" are the stars of a new form of show biz, showing up on television with an imposing entourage.

In addition to these sociological observations, the observation of player behavior the world over, and in particular in Japan and Korea, gives a completely different feel to this form of expression. "Addictive" behaviors (see (Seys, 2003) and (Griffiths, 2005) for an analysis of this fashionable and ill-defined term) have been observed. This is also the case for users of single-player games and the Internet. Here, however, it is easy to perceive the psychological risk resulting from the practice of MMOG's. A player may be a cashier in a supermarket or his supervisor's punching-bag during the day, and every evening the prince of a universe—fictional, of course, but whose subjects are indeed real. It is easy to see which part of his life will soon enough become the most important.

This example leads to a positive observation already made by several psychologists (Stora, 2005): if someone is able to be the leader of thousands of peoples in a virtual world, even if he only knows them though their avatars, his job in the real world, a cashier in a supermarket, is probably a waste of his abilities. The use of online games as social training and evaluation models has already been experimented with. The next step is to build online cooperative activities adapted to people who may have some problems in classical communication environments and are much more comfortable with online systems.

Network games encourage positive social behaviors in other way, as well. Like chatrooms, they are generally spaces for socialization. Encounters on the Internet often end up leading to encounters in real life (IRL). The game provides a means of comprehending and participating in the creation of a society and an economy. It is a means of expression and creation, and will be to a greater and greater extent as the possibilities grow for the utilization and free transformation of game objects by the player. In the manner of MUD's and of many virtual communities on the Internet, there are a growing number of persistent games to be found which have an associative or artistic origin. Let us cite two examples: *Le Deuxième Monde* (*The Second World*) was an experiment, on the boundary between virtual communities and games, which was developed by Cryo and Canal+. The space of *The Second World* was a virtual version of Paris that served as a meeting space for the game. Abandoned by the publisher for diverse economic reasons, this space has been taken up again by a collective community (Galibert, 2003). There are many artistic experiments that derive from virtual communities (Balpe 2000). In the set of games *Society*, Bruno Samper and the team at Panoplie experiment with short meeting experiences through strange avatars in universes related to artistic archetypes. "From our point of view, video games are the most relevant form of creation in the twenty-first century. *Society* is, in some way, a manifest of this vision." (http://www.panoplie.fr)

Is an MMOG still a video game? It resembles many single-player games, but neither the objectives nor the gameplay are of the same type. Rather, it resembles a board game, and in particular role-playing board games, but the players do not meet each other physically in a given place for a given length of time. It resembles Internet chat rooms, with communication accomplished in the same fashion, but with the discussions between participants relating to an interactive fiction conceived and controlled by the game designer. It resembles a television program, a televirtual game show, with its winners and losers, but the audience is also in the game. Depending on the angle from which they are viewed, MMOG's collect and combine all forms of communication that may be found in broadcast and Internet media.

Proactive, Mobile, Ubiquitous, ... Games Everywhere

Technology Evolution

The next generation of games uses two major technological evolutions: the cross-media platform and the distribution of intelligent sensors and actuators.

The cross-media platform provides a general high-level interface for distributed applications using various types of digital terminals (computers, mobile phones, PDA's, interactive TV's, etc.). It is, of course, the high-level interface of mobile telecommunication services and the user view of the integration of communication networks. The cross-media platform should provide a great variety of services related to content and automatic interface adaptation, user and group identification, spatial localization, security, etc. When you use your mobile phone to read your mail or view a web page, to pay at a parking lot or movie theater, you are using the basic function of the cross-media platform.

The second technology, related to the previous one, is the ability to spread intelligent computer sensors and actuators in all possible locations. These devices are connected and become an intelligent system able to understand the user's situation and needs everywhere and at any time. It is able to react according to the user's current needs. This technology is often referred to as ubiquitous computing. The distribution of sensors relies mainly on the use of real-time image and sound recognition: using distributed digital video cameras, the system can understand gestures or even the user's emotions. The PlayStation 2 EyeToys games are a good example of this technology. But all of our everyday objects can be transformed into intelligent sensors: the sofa can detect in which position you want to rest, the shutter at what time you open it, the coffee machine how much coffee and water you like, etc. For example, mobile-phone systems are able to compute your location. The same technology can be applied to actuators. Sensors, actuators, small processors, and wireless interfaces can be combined into "smart objects."

These technologies lead to a new level of interaction between real and virtual worlds: the intelligent and distributed applications manage an image of the real world and are able to directly interact asynchronously with the real world.

Of course, the application of the cross-media platform and ubiquitous computing is not limited to games, but games have been one of the first type of applications able to use these technologies as the basis of new content and communication modes.

The Return of the War of the Worlds

Starting from the unified platform, it is possible to imagine a new generation of massively multiplayer games in which, through mobile phones, personal digital assistants, computers, televisions, etc., the player stays in constant contact with the game universe.

He can receive messages from his avatar, from other players, even from the game engine. He can search for clues to help him in his quest in "real world" media. On the other hand, a radio or television station may continually broadcast news on the state of the virtual universe. The player could, in the skin of his avatar, be the commander of another realm or a Mafia godfather. He could have a small virtual family that wishes him a happy birthday with more punctuality than his real family. Permanently connected to the virtual universe by an entire panoply of appliances, the player could interact with the game world using all of the interfaces at his disposal: from the keyboard of his mobile telephone to the joystick of his console. What characterizes this type of game are interactions between the player and the virtual universe that are not formally distinguishable from interactions with the real world through media (radio, television, web, newspapers), telecommunications systems (phone, mail, video conferences), and the use of everyday objects. For scripting, this has the consequence that proactive games do not take place in a medieval world—whose day-to-day interactions with the real world would be difficult to make a case for—but are rather in the realm of contemporary fiction. However, imagination is key, and the player may be a contemporary representative of time-traveling

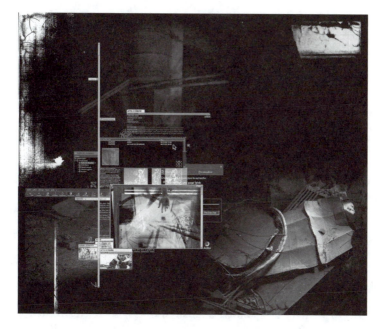

In Memoriam (Lexis Numérique/Ubisoft, 2003).

agents, which would justify the interactions perfectly well. Giving to the player the role of a "time guardian," he can be responsible for holding enemies from the past and the future in check.

Proactive games are not some distant utopia; they have already been experimented with in various forms. One of the first examples is the game *Majestic*. This game, released by Electronic Arts in 2000, has as its goal the foiling of a plot targeting the United States, within a universe largely inspired by *The X-Files* television series. The player must subscribe and register through the Internet onto a database that furnishes him—through email, fax, or phone—hints for his investigation. He must also pursue this investigation on certain websites. The game is not limited in time, since, following the principle of serials, a new episode was offered every month. In 2002, the publisher abandoned *Majestic* because of an insufficient clientele. In 2003, Ubisoft published *In Memoriam*, a game written by Éric Viennot and developed by Lexis Numérique (and later rereleased under the title *Missing*). The principle here is very similar; the investigation is now concerned with the disappearance of two journalists. The clues must be either found on the web (in particular, on the site for the newspaper *Libération*) or are sent in the form of email. In this case, the game as it was sold had only one ending. However, in both cases, the games have escaped their designers: virtual communities continue the adventures, creating new clues in the stories, which grow more and more complex.

The two preceding games are advanced example of alternate reality games (ARG's). During the last three years, using less technology, numerous ARG's have been launched on the web. They use the idea of a puzzle that has to be solved using clues spread out over the Internet. The game relies on a collaboration between players who communicate through instant messages and email. They are often free to play and linked to a marketing operation. One of the most famous ARG's is *The Beast*, whose design principles are describe by Sean Stewart (http://www.seanstewart.org/beast/intro/):

> On January 2–4, 2001, a small and very secret team met in the offices of Microsoft's Game Group to plan and design a massive, web-based scavenger-hunt/soap opera. For years Jordan Weisman had been thinking about doing a game that would be sort of like the Beatles Paul-Is-Dead mystery—an elaborate web of clues and possible conspiracies to be investigated by a huge group of fans.
>
> The internet supplied the medium—a place where you could deliver a ton of content, and be assured that players would talk about it with one another. As for the message, the games group had been given the challenge of creating a virtual world to stand behind the new Spielberg movie, *A.I.* Spielberg and his producer, Kathy Kennedy, felt that *A.I.*'s themes made it only natural that the movie's life should expand not in sequels, but on computer. So far, so good.
>
> Jordan's vision was based on a series of assumptions.
>
> 1. *The narrative would be broken into fragments, which the players would be required to reassemble.* That is,

the players, like the advanced robots at the end of the movie, would be doing something essentially archaeological, combing through the welter of life in the 22nd century, to piece a story together out of fragments.

2. *The game would—of necessity—be fundamentally cooperative and collective, because of the nature of the Internet.* His belief, which we all shared, was that if we put a clue in a Turkish newspaper at dawn, it would be under discussion in a high school kid's basement in Iowa by dinner time.

3. *The game would be cooler if nobody knew who was doing it, or why.* Therefore, secrecy was very tight. Almost nobody at Microsoft would know what the hell we were doing. Jordan had brought in old pal Pete Fenlon to subcontract writers, artists, and web designers, for the sake of speed and staying under MS's own internal radar.

4. *The game would be cooler if it came at you, through as many different conduits as possible.* Websites. E-mails. Phone calls. Newspaper clippings. Faxes. SMS messaging. TV spots. Smoke signals. Whalesong.

In an earlier conversation, Jordan had been sitting around mulling the idea over with Elan Lee, when his phone rang. He glanced at Elan, grinning. "Wouldn't it be cool if that was the game calling"

The next level of interaction between the real and the virtual world is provided by localized "ubigames" (ubiquitous games). The MMOG *Mogi* (NewtGame, 2003) and *BotFighters 2* (Alive Mobile Games, 2000) are good examples in this category. They are both location-based mobile multiplayer games. The scenario of *Mogi* is simply to seek and collect virtual objects with a mobile phone. The objects are virtually distributed in a real town, and the player must physically move to find them using the location function of mobile phones. The goal is to accumulate points by collecting objects. *Botfighters 2* is a location-based action FPS MMOG. The player has to attack other players with his mobile phone while moving in the streets of a town, stealing secret information, destroying the enemy's installations, etc. The main interface is the phone, but some actions can be performed on a standard PC over the Internet. The sensor is the phone system and its location capability, but some information (the weather in the town) is taken from various sources on the Internet.

In BotFighter, the TV is not always used and is not the main interface of the game. The next step is to use a mix of the TV broadcast channel and the network interactivity possibility in a single game. It is the future of interactive TV as soon as some standard interface for TV set-top boxes is adapted. There are already several examples of interactive-TV game experiments.

In 2000, Kalisto was developing a technology that allowed a television viewer of a sports match to participate virtually in the competition.

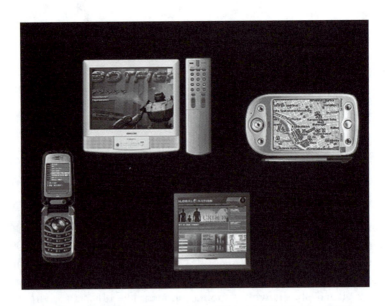

Interfaces of the *BotFighters 2* game (Alive Mobile Games, 2000).

You are watching a Formula 1 grand prix race, when you suddenly find yourself flying off in a virtual race car, which runs the track with Schumacher's Ferrari. Of course you win, which is a great satisfaction, even if Schumacher will never know it. Since Kalisto eventually went bankrupt, it was unable to complete the experiment. However, this was certainly some of the most interesting work in the impending mixture between real and virtual worlds.

In 2002, the French TV channel group Canal+ launched *Piktorezo*, a multiplayer interactive-TV game. Collective interaction relies on the ability to exchange instant messages between spectators during play. Other interactive programs allow the viewers to watch a sporting event through individually chosen camera. For example, NASCAR allows racing fans to view races from inside one of seven cars participating in a race. The viewer can watch his favorite driver's face during a race and can see him pressing the gas pedal. Using his TV remote control, the viewer can also jump from one car to another.

Conclusion

This chapter is certainly the most prognostic of the book. If it is no longer certain that an MMOG, and, a fortiori, a proactive game, is a video game, it is difficult to predict developments in this field and their social, economic, and scientific implications.

The relative economic weakness of MMOG's and proactive games may be attributed to an immaturity in both supply and demand. *World of Warcraft* (a notable exception) is a great commercial success. One may search for another audience in other universes. Alternate reality games show the way: the game must be a fiction embedded in everyday life. One of the main issues that has been addressed in this chapter is the construction of semantic relationships between the real and virtual worlds. The trading of virtual goods in MMOG's is a fist step. The asynchronous call of the game to the player, using standard phones and mails, is the second step. When the game knows the location of the player and can interact with him through smart objects, the boundary of the two worlds becomes evanescent. The building of global relationships between the two worlds, related to the weather, political events, or sporting events, constitutes the next step in this integration process.

The importance of this type of game will be revealed to the extent that it approaches conventional media and leaves the domain of video games in the current sense of the term. One can imagine a special newsletter or a television magazine that reports the current events of virtual worlds, and perhaps even a VCNN (Virtual CNN) channel dedicated uniquely to fake wars, in which everybody may participate through an intermediary mobile device. As real wars are sometimes presented through a 3D graphics simulation, the confusion between real and virtual events may become total. The narrative and spectacular presentation of television news as it is presently practiced, facilitates this transition. The integration of different methods of audiovisual production is also headed in this direction. Ten years from now, at most, the development of telecommunication infrastructure will supply the majority of western and southeast Asian living rooms with high-speed networks, with or without wires, supplying a mixture of phone, television, and Internet. The users of this infrastructure will be ripe for a new type of media, as will be the producers and creators.

The confusion between real and virtual information, and the possibility for it to successfully occur, already has a long history. Orson Welles made his mark in 1937 by giving one of the most famous radio broadcasts ever, which supplies a model of the genre. He announced, in the style of American radio news flashes, an invasion by Martians, provoking a monster panic.[1] Proactive games constitute a grand return of the *War of the Worlds* in the Internet era.

Because this new interweaving of real and virtual may be frightening, it would be foolish to content ourselves with cursing the sorcerer's apprentices, who may indeed unleash something beyond their control. The active elements in the field of network games shall have in their hands the writing methods of tomorrow, as well as the science and technology of a century that will be dominated to a great extent by the issues of communication. To stay outside of the race is suicidal. To participate, on the contrary, will allow one to understand the rules and, thus, allow one to modify them.

---

[1] It is interesting to listen to this broadcast, which has been published in the form of a CD-ROM by Radio France and the INA. The Woody Allen film *Radio Days* relates, among other things, this episode from the history of radio.

- 4 -

Video-Game Technologies

Introduction

In this chapter, we give a succinct presentation of game technologies, the features that distinguish them from those used in other multimedia fields, and their short-term and medium-term development.

The figure on the following page schematically shows the mechanisms of production and display for a game. The top of the figure represents game production: the manufacture of the game world's constituent objects and programming of the dynamic behaviors that define the evolution of these objects as a function of the spectator's actions. The bottom of the figure represents what happens when a player is using the game. This process is a simulation that synthesizes, or generates, the images and sounds that the player perceives as a function of his actions.

What characterizes a game, and more generally a virtual reality system, is the fact that the image and sound must be generated in real time, that is to say, in time with the player's perceptions. This requirement limits the comparative complexity of the calculations that a computer or game console may perform. In contrast, the production of an animated film may follow nearly the same scheme; however, since the spectator does not intervene in the film, it is possible to use several hours of computer time to synthesize a few minutes of film.

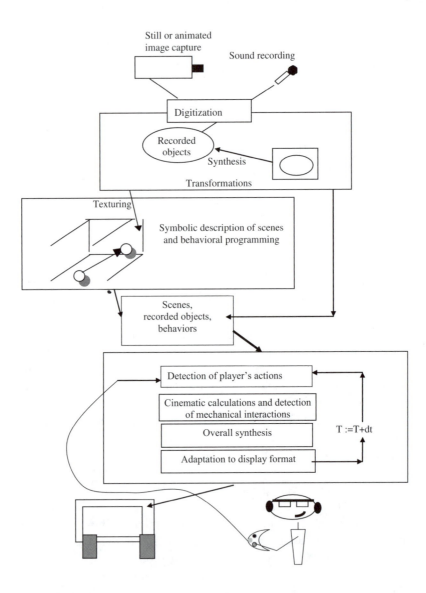

Mechanisms of production and display.

A simulation system used for training, like those used to teach the piloting of an airplane, has the same constraints as a game; it, however, relies on very costly and specific technology.

Video games face the challenge of generating complex images and sounds of high quality in real time, and to do all this on relatively inexpensive computers. These constraints determine the technologies that are depicted at the bottom of the schematic, involving synthesis in real time. The top part, that is to say, game manufacture properly speaking, is affected by the limits that are imposed on the design and production of the objects—an object may not have the same structure, the same realism, in a game as in a film. The behavior of an enemy cannot be as complex in a game as it is in a military training simulator. The tools used to produce the objects in a game are thus very close to those employed for audiovisual post-production and simulator programming. It is their manner of implementation that is specific to games.

We will discuss the operations described in the figure in more detail. At the first stage, graphic artists, videographers, and musicians create the digital materials: scanned images, videos, and sound in a digital format. We call these (visual or sonic) elements *textures*. There are two possible procedures for constructing these materials: either recording the image or sound, or creating them from a mathematical model. In either case, one obtains a file that is a digitized image, video, or sound. It is then possible to apply various digital transformations to these data. In the second stage, one must construct a symbolic representation of the game's universe. By using a modeler like 3ds Max or Maya, a graphic artist designs the 3D objects through composition operations using simple forms or as a structure composed of polygons.

He then adds detail to the objects by covering them with a texture, which is, for example, an image file designed during the first stage. He places the objects within the game space, as well as placing the virtual light sources and the initial positions of the cameras. He describes the animations that do not depend on the player's actions. For example, these could be the animations that represent a character who is waiting, running, or throwing a punch. The ensemble of these animations make up one of the attributes of the character that are used within the game. All of this is similar to the creative work in animated films and uses

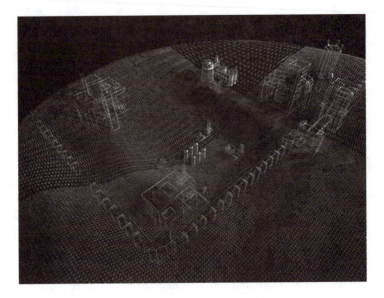

A landscape in the process of development, showing its polygonal structure (*Genetic Warriors* project, DESS JVMI and the author, 2002).

the same tools, within the limits set by the requirement of real-time synthesis.

The sound undergoes the same treatment: it can be represented by an audio file recorded in the first phase or by a symbolic MIDI file (play an *A* on the piano for 20 milliseconds with a loud attack). The tools used are those of audio postproduction: synthesizers, sequencers, and mixing tools like Sonic Foundry, ProTools, etc.

The programmers begin by describing, in a suitable computer language (C++ for PC/console games, Java for mobile-phone games), the behavior of each object, which depends on the player and on the possible interactions with other objects. Then, they link objects to behaviors and integrate the various elements of the universe. To accomplish, this they use specific software called the *game engine*, which supplies all of the basic functions required for real-time synthesis. Finally, the level designers program, in a specialized language (known as script language), the game's interactive scenario. This language uses as its basic operations the object behavior that has been created by the programmers.

The bottom of the figure describes, in a very simplified way (Rollings, 2003), (Sanchez-Crespau Dalmau, 2004), what the *monitor*—the program which pilots the game—does when the player plays. It cyclically executes the following actions:

- it detects the commands entered by the player in the preceding cycle;

- it evaluates their effects on the objects, while executing the corresponding script elements;

- it calculates the displacement of objects and determines the interactions, such as collisions, between different objects;

- with everything now placed virtually, including the eyes and ears of the player's avatar, the monitor synthesizes the image and sound as they should be perceived;

- the image is posted to the screen and the sound sent to the speakers.

The length of a cycle is set by the frequency of image refreshment, from 15 to 60 images per second depending on the platform. This frequency determines the fluidity of animation.

In this chapter, we discuss the problems tied to the treatment of the image, then of the sound, and finally of artificial intelligence. We present the structure of a game engine and address the problems inherent in game networks. A part of this chapter is taken from (Natkin, 2003).

Image Technology

Roughly speaking, imaging technology for games corresponds to that used in computer animation, with a time lag of five to ten years. In other words, a game graphics engine of today can fabricate in real time what animation software was able to do in the early mid-nineties. The fluidity of animation and the quality of image rendering are key elements of games, since the player compares what he sees in the game to what he could see in a film. The following table shows the average percentages of computing power allocated to the different functions of a game in 2000 (Gal, 2000). It illustrates the emphasis on graphic functions.

Platform	Graphics	Sound	AI and Other
PC	60	15	25
Console	75	15	10

Towards the beginning of the nineties, the majority of games offered a flat (2D) universe in which the camera moved solely by horizontal displacements, or viewed the universe from above. Today, most PC and console games make use of a 3D universe. Games on portable consoles, PDAs, and mobile phones are themselves at the level of console games from around 1995. This has led to the development of high-performance graphics processors, integrated first into PC's and then into game consoles.

3D engines have two main functions: the animation (cinematic) computation, that is to say the determination of an object's trajectory and the real-time rendering, i.e., the synthesis of the image as it is seen by the player.

Creating animation in games is still a large problem in terms of complexity and costs. Most animation in games is based on the same technique as 3D movie animation: key frame. Using a 3D design tool like 3ds Max or Maya, the graphic designer builds a 3D model of a character. The trajectories of the key points of the model are computed either step by step, applying translation or rotations of each part of the body (forward kinematics) or by an interpolation between the final and initial positions of the limbs (inverse kinematics). To obtain nice characters and animations, in particular for human and realistic animals, this process is far from being fully automated and requires the intervention of numerous clever graphic designers and animators. They produce a precomputed animation which is used, during game execution, by the 3D engine to apply three types of transformation in real time: interpolation between two successive animations, mixing of two simultaneous animations (animation blending) and real-time coordinate transformation. If we consider a character who runs, coordinate transformation is used to change the character's direction and the mixing of animations is used to superpose the animation of the head and the animation of the legs. When the character stops running, its position is interpolated between the last running position and the initial position of a new animation. Precomputed animations can also be obtained using motion capture (mocap). Mocap has been used for 15 years in noninteractive animation and is becoming more and more popular in games, as its cost and technical complexity have greatly decreased. Motion capture relies on the recording of the trajectories of key points of a real object. For example, an actor goes through the required movements to animate a humanoid character. Different technologies can be used to records trajectories (magnet or infrared sensors, for example), but the use of cameras placed around the object is the more common technology. As with key-frame animation, the results must be controlled and refined by an animator. In any case, key frame or mocap, a good professional needs from one to three days to make a simple animation. Thinking about a cowboy character, many animations may be needed: riding, drinking, walking, sitting in a chair, dying, etc. And since the cowboy may sit in the chair with varying starting poses, as many animations as initial poses have to be created.

To resolves this problem, a new type of animation technique, physical animation, is more frequently used. *Physical animation* is the animation that is obtained by a simulation of the physical laws that draw the object. For example, in an FPS, many nonplayer characters (NPC's) die and they die beginning in numerous initial positions. These may include, for example, the position of the character when the bullet hits him, etc. Physical characteristics (weight, freedom of movement) are assigned to each part of the character's body. In real time, the game engine simulates the effect of gravity, leading to a more realistic real-time animation that works for any initial position. Physical animation is not, strictly speaking, a part of the 3D engine but rather a part of the physical engine. Physical animation may be used for cloth animations, particle systems, etc. The physical engine can compute the trajectory of a ball or the realistic relation of skis on snow in sports games, the explosion of a car crashing into a wall, or the hole in a wall made by a bullet. Games like *Half-Life 2* are famous for how the player may manipulate almost all of the objects in the game. For example, the player can take a bottle and throw it against a wall. The resulting animation is com-

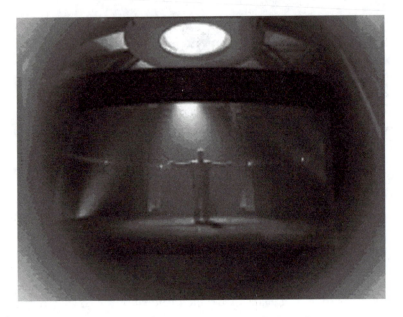

The Cyberdome: a motion-capture system (XD productions).

puted by the physical engine. Physical simulation is starting to be used
for other functions of the game engine, for example, to synthesize Foley
effects (the sound of the bottle crashing on the wall). There are two
main differences between physical animation in games and that used in
industrial systems (such as industrial flight simulators): the game platform has limited computing power and the results of the simulation in
games needs to be spectacular, but not necessarily accurate.

At the boundary between 3D-engine and physical-engine functions
is the detection of collisions between virtual objects. It is the main
source of internal events which drives a game"s behavior as the bound-
aries of object motion (for example, walls) are computed in real time by
collision detection.

Real-time rendering is the computation of the image as it is seen by
the player. The input data of the renderer is the geometry of all objects
in the scene and their positions, the position and characteristics of light
sources, the characteristics and position of the virtual camera, and the
set of textures that "covers" an object. Textures are bit-mapped images

that are used for several purposes: simulating material aspects, small deformations, etc.

The sequence of operations needed to compute an image is called the graphics pipeline (Akenine-Moller, 2002). It includes the geometry stage that is in charge of the analysis of the relative position of objects with regard to the camera, and the computation of the lighting equation that defines the color of each element in the scene. The transformation of this abstract scene into a map of pixel colors is done by the second part of the pipeline, the rasterizing stage. The image below includes the initial animation computation stage.

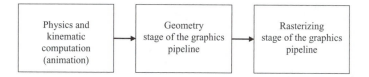

Image-processing pipeline.

The main difference between the graphics pipeline in games and in noninteractive animation is related to the lighting computation. Offline rendering uses both a global model of illumination, like ray tracing or radiosity, and a local computation. A global algorithm takes into account the global geometry of the scene. For example, the ray-tracing algorithm recursively computes the path of light rays from virtual light sources to the eye of the spectator, taking into account the successive reflections of the light on objects. This kind of algorithm is able to compute realistic lighting and shadowing effects but is CPU-intensive consuming and, currently, cannot be executed in real time. A local model applies a lighting model to small parts of objects (polygons, vertices, or pixels) taking into account the light source and the camera position. Research and practice in the area of algorithms for game graphics focus on technical subterfuge to simulate global effects using a local model. The computation for local models is less CPU-intensive than for global models, and it can be executed on a dedicated graphics processing unit (GPU). This method was first used to simulate dynamic shadowing; that is, shadows that change in real time with the light and the object's motion. For example, local models of lighting and dynamic texture mapping that include the image of the shadow are applied to each triangle. The same idea has been extended to simulate other visual effects leading to the notion of vertex and pixel shaders according to the granularity of the model. The results are sometime so impressive that the same techniques are now used also in noninteractive animations.

Another area under development in computer graphics for games is the use of real-time procedural images. This is directly related to generativity which is described later in this chapter. For example, a procedural texture is a bit-mapped image that is generated by a program. The use of such a texture has two advantages. First, bit-mapped textures generally represent a large volume of information, whereas procedural textures are defined by a short program. The second advantage is that, if the program includes some random information, it can generates an almost infinite number of textures of the same kind.

The new generation of consoles (Xbox 360, PlayStation 3, Nintendo Revolution) will have at its disposal impressive computational capacities in general, and graphic capabilities in particular. One may therefore imagine that the race towards realistic synthesis will progress at the same speed. However, this is not certain, since the present level of technology already offers very high image quality, and some players prefer an improvement of gameplay over one of graphics. Likewise, through other influences, such as *manga* (Japanese comics), the aesthetic of certain games abandons 3D realism in favor of a graphic style lifted from abstraction, comic books, 2D animation, or video. It is interesting in this regard to consult games such as *Rez, The Legend of Zelda: The Wind Waker, XIII*, and *In Memoriam*.

Research in the matter of image synthesis is not highly connected to games. It focuses on techniques of scene representation and realistic rendering that will not be feasible for real time use for a few years. On the other hand, games are starting to demand analysis techniques, for images and sounds created in real time that allow for the integration of information coming from the real world into the game—namely, the face and voice of the player. Finally, at the boundary between image synthesis and artificial intelligence is research into the future development of characters with convincing attitudes and expressions, with the ability to discover their virtual environments.

XIII (Ubisoft, 2003).

Sound Technology

The essential choices in the matter of sound, including the architecture of the three components (music, voices, and sound effects) and their relationship to game structure and to the images, are defined during the phase of game design (Gal, 2002). Unfortunately, the sound is generally integrated into the game only at the end of production, when all the graphics have been constructed. The sound designer must therefore prepare all of the sonic elements without being able to test them before the final stage of production of each game level.

Sound is an essential factor for immersion in the game. It is thus necessary, in a framework that escapes temporal control, to continually refresh audio elements. Sound effects are more frequently either transformed or synthesized in real time. This allows, for example, variation in the sound of a footstep as a function of the ground stepped on, and an almost imperceptible variation in its rhythm. Spoken dialogue (as opposed to the textual dialogue common in current games) is used to a greater and greater extent. Starting from a conventional recording, the challenge consists in varying the intonation as a function of the acoustics of different locations and the circumstances of the dialogue. The technology for treating the former factor is currently available. On the other hand, real-time transformation of vocal intonation is still a subject of research.

The most complex part of sonic design is the construction of interactive music. Film music is strongly marked by dramatics. In a game, music is tied to the space. Most present-day game designers associate a sound loop with each location in a given level. These loops must then be modified in real time to manage the transitions between scenes. The techniques of transition rely either on classic harmonic principles or on sound-mixing techniques (Harland, 2000).

It may be said that we are entering into a third period in the development of sound within games. The first generation of games, supported on cartridges with read-only memory (ROM), like the Nintendo NES, for example, did not allow for storage of recorded sound. The music and sound effects were defined in symbolic fashion (similar to MIDI) and generated by the console synthesizer. This produced a type of characteristic music (Nintendo music) that one may still hear on a Game Boy—fairly exasperating for some people, but it has its fans.

The revolution came with the arrival of CD-ROM support on consoles and PC's. It then became possible to store high-quality audio. To control the processor-load and memory allocated to the sound, synthesis and transformations are limited to the minimum necessary for managing the interactivity. With this goal, the sonic designer plays with a mix of many channels in real time (48 channels for the PS2), produced by dedicated hardware. The sound design of the majority of present games rests on these principles. The soundtracks of the games *GTA 3*, *Jak and Daxter*, and *Silent Hill 2* are examples of this second period.

However, a new approach is beginning to be used, in particular for PC games. New capabilities and the use of powerful sound cards, like the Sound Blaster of Creative Labs, allow the reintroduction of sound treatment and synthesis in real time. As a first step, this involves simulating the acoustics and location of the objects producing the sound. The player, given a helmet or a 5.1 sound system, hears the bullets whistling overhead, and the voice of the monster is much more cavernous in a cave than at the seaside. Furthermore, the appearance of standards for synthesis techniques (using wave tables) allows a musician to control, in a much more precise way, the generation of music on the PC. This gives rise to the possibility of truly interactive, eventually generative, music for games. The soundtrack of a game like *Rez* is an example of the promising aspects of this evolution.

As with image processing, the principles of algorithms used in real-time synthesis and sound transformation are well known. The difficulty is to execute these transformations in real time within a game console or a PC (Cook, 2002). Another issue is the development of authoring tools for games. During the last decade, several products have been proposed without much success. Microsoft DirectMusic Producer is an example of one such tool: it is a very complete and complex real-time sound editor that relies on the Microsoft DirectX sound API and that is based on the classical principles of music composition—The composer proposes a melody, then a harmonization, and at the end an orchestration. At each step, several variations can be proposed or generated. The one that is chosen in real time can depend either on game events or on random parameters. As the sample used can be music or Foley effects, in principle, the same tool can be used for sound design. It seems that this musical metaphor was too far from methods used by game sound designers.

The new generation of tools is much simpler. The Microsoft proposal is called XSACT and the CreativeLabs tool is entitled ISACT. The similarity is not only in the names; the two tools are basically real-time mixers and sequencers, i.e., they allow you to program the ordering and the merging of several sound sources coming either from audio samples or from MIDI files. They both allow the application of real-time transformations, in particular reverberation and spacialization of the sound, and the creation of random and event-dependent sound mixes. An interface with the game dynamic, through events and transitions, is supplied. The software FMOD Ex (Firelight Technologies) has fewer features but has two great advantages: the use for noncommercial applications is free, and it works on 12 platforms, including game consoles.

In sonic matters, gaming research is essentially concerned with generative music, which we introduce later in this chapter; the synthesis and expressivity of voices, allowing the transformation of dialogue as a function of differing situations; and the improvement of virtual acoustic techniques and sound spatialization.

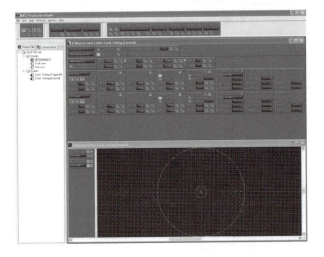

The audio-sample interface of ISACT (CreativeLabs) .

Artificial Intelligence

There are areas of information science which, having been neglected after an intense period of research and disappointing potential applications, find in video games, and more generally in virtual worlds, a remarkable opportunity for experimentation and development. Artificial intelligence and game theory are two examples. Something that only works with great difficulty in a very complex, real world will sometimes work much better in a virtual universe whose rules are designed, controlled, and modified with little trouble. In the longer term, persistent games offer a hope for economists, urban planners, and sociologists to find a world where their predictions are realized and, above all, a space where social experimentation, in the sense of the so-called hard sciences, can be performed.

To understand these opportunities, let us recall one of the most fundamental challenges of artificial intelligence. To the question of how to recognize, if it happens one day, that a computer is intelligent, the famous mathematician Alan Turing proposed, in 1950, a response that is in principle very simple, called the *Turing test* (Saygin, 2000), or *imitation game*. We start with two closed rooms, placing a human in one and a computer in the other. An investigator, who doesn't know which room holds the person and which the machine, can pose a set of questions to both of them, with no limits on subject or complexity, using a computer terminal, for example. The questions and responses are analyzed by a jury. The day when the jury will no longer be able to deduce from the responses which room contains the computer, the computer can be considered intelligent.

This test has given rise to innumerable discussions and polemics. A contest (the Loebner Prize) is held periodically. We direct the reader to the reference cited above and to the innumerable publications on the subject that can be found on the Internet. Let's return to video games.

Suppose that we limit the test in the following fashion: the human and the computer are both involved in a master video game, one through an avatar and the other as a nonplayer character (NPC). The two positions are interchangeable within the game. Moreover, the computer that runs the game (if there is one) is not the same as the one that plays and does not know who controls the avatar and who controls the NPC. The jury observes the game. The day when the jury is unable to distinguish the avatar from the NPC, the computer will play like a human.

This does not imply that the computer plays either better or worse than the human; instead, it means that it has human-type behavior. This doesn't prove anything much about the intelligence of the computer, but on the other hand, it is of considerable interest within the framework of gaming and of the creation of a credible virtual universe. At this point, it is important to distinguish what researchers and practitioners mean by "artificial intelligence." Video-game professionals have taken the Turing test to the very letter and give the name "artificial intelligence" to any technique that allows a game to not give the impression of being too stupid. In video games, artificial intelligence is all in appearances.

Finally, to finish this introduction, let us note that it is today possible to write a program that can play chess in a way that is very difficult to differentiate from that of a human, which is what Turing effectively envisaged in his original article.

In a video game, artificial intelligence (AI) comes into play on several levels. To begin with, it manages the relationships between characters and their environments. The most classic example of this is the search for a path that allows one to reach a given place from the current position (*path finding*). The method used to accomplish this must, at a minimum, allow obstacles to be avoided. It can search for a path either in the map or in the game space. It may have other constraints, depending on the game's genre and the situation. For example, in a game of stealth or warfare, a path must be found in which the character is out of cover for as little time as possible. Finally, the progression along the path must be "human," which is to say, not too robotic, if the character is human. Path finding applies to the NPC's, but also, in certain strategy games, for example, to the characters controlled by the player. In the latter, when the player wants to direct one of the armies under his command, he contents himself with specifying the destination. In general, the troops acquiesce with a "Yes, sir!" which is as feeble as it is exasperated, and they leave towards their destination, following the path calculated by the computer. This relationship with the environment generalizes to more complex problems, for example, how to detect an object like a chair or a staircase and intelligently manage the geometry of the character so that he may seem to utilize these objects like a human would.

The second level at which AI comes into play concerns the behavior of individuals. How should one manage the NPC of the temple guard so that he acts effectively, at least in appearance, when the avatar, Harrison Ford in person, presents himself? If Harrison is in the apparent axis of the guard's vision, the guard is required to at least fire at him. If Harrison fires and misses him, the guard must duck for cover and continue to fire, and so on.

The third level concerns collective behaviors. They begin with the management of character movements (behavior of individuals within a crowd, movement of military units and planes in formation) and extend up to the tactical behaviors in strategy games or team sports games.

The fourth level concerns strategy and only affects puzzle-type games or games of evolved strategies. It supposes a minimum amount of training of player behavior.

The fifth level poses the problem of interactive narrative: how to adapt the course of the game to the behavior of the player. The relation with training may be implicit. The computer knows the player's journey and evaluates his abilities. As a consequence, it manages the level of difficulty, the expression of dramatic intensity, etc. The relation may also be explicit: the player manages a system of apprenticeship. For example, in *Black & White*, the player tames a creature through a system of reward and punishment. This creature is then indispensable to him for defeating other gods, and if it is not docile or combative enough, the player is handicapped.

From this short description, it is easy to determine the areas that have a connection with gaming AI, either as sources or borrowers of techniques. For example, the first three levels are tied to robotics (the movement and behavior of a robot or a group of robots) and to animation (the creation of scenes by generative mechanisms). The fourth level is one of the fundamental aspects of AI in general, and of expert systems in particular. The fifth level raises the problem of expression in interactive media. The applications for computer-assisted educational materials are innumerable.

Taking an analytical viewpoint of human psychology, artificial intelligence behavior is divided into three functions: perception, decision, and action. The mainly AI implements the first two functions, and the action is performed by other modules of the game engine. This scheme has to be considered at several levels of a hierarchy. The following example (Reynolds 2004) analyzes the AI of team membership in FPS games like *Halo*. The decision is based on the following levels of rules, by decreasing order of priority:

1. **Player level.** The player must be able to play the game, and the team management must help him, but not too much, as the player is the hero. This can be translated into rules like: "The first priority of an NPC is to stay out of the player's way .... NPC teammates should select their weapons according to the player's current weaponry. It would not be much fun for a player to be outgunned by his teammates." The perception of the NPC is the knowledge of the player's position, direction velocity, and current weaponry. The decision process selects paths and weapons according to the preceding rules.

2. **Threat level.** The role of an NPC is to help the player in his fight against enemies. A rule of this level might be: "The NPC should

always look for a target. If a target is suspected and the team is too busy to provide backup, the target should be engaged." The perception detects targets, and then a set of decision rules are applied.

3. **Environment level.** "This layer causes NPC's to consider their surroundings and behave correctly and tactically within this environment .... The NPC should use anything that can be used to cover and avoid area that is too exposed ...." The perception must find protected and open areas. This leads to path-finding decisions.

4. **Team Manager.** The decision of each teammate should be consistent with the decision of other NPC's in the team. For example, "the global rate of fire should be controlled to avoid having multiple NPC's run out of ammunition simultaneously."

Such AI policy is an important element of the game AI goals: AI should be a support to the gameplay, the goal of which is to make the game fun for the player (levels 1 and 2); the AI must provide credible behavior (levels 3 and 4).

In games, the perception and action functions are simpler to implement than in real-life applications. The perception function is an adaptation and an efficient formatting of the game universe that can be, in theory, perfectly known. For example, the vision function of a robot working in a factory is dependent on sensors and a complex analysis and filtering of the captured data. The vision function of an NPC is the determination of which game objects he is able to see, according to the game design. At a low level, for example, path finding, the perception function relies on an a priori analysis of the game world and the composition of a model of this world dedicated to AI function. For example, the topology and possible NPC paths can be stored in this model. The following figure shows the path editor of the Kynapse software developed by Kynogon.

The decision function is still the most difficult function to implement. A decision is related to an environment and a knowledge that has to be implemented as a real-time data base. In a game, all of the objects and behavior that have to be in this database can be perfectly known and

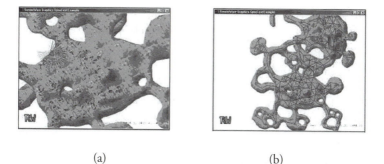

(a)   (b)

Pathdata: (a) Automatic generation; (b) editing.

recorded, since they rely on the history and state of the game. But the management of such data can be too complex and resource-intensive to be handled in real time on a game platform. Then the decision algorithm, by itself, must not be too complex as its predictability and efficiency in terms of gameplay and credibility can become untestable. So most games use a technique called scripted AI, which is not really AI in the academic meaning of the term. Scripted AI is a set of decision rules, like the one presented in the preceding example, that are implemented in the game as a part of the game code as statements related to the current state of the game. To avoid predictability, some rules may have several decision outputs that are chosen randomly.

Individual and collective behavior is described in the form of local or global automaton: the temple guard's development is programmed either within a global script, which describes the scenario to be followed when Harrison enters the temple zone, or as part of an ensemble of scripts that describe what each character must do. Such an ensemble is relatively rudimentary and relies on the principle that after two or three momentary setbacks, Harrison will necessarily enter the temple and will not return later to see if the intelligence of the guards has progressed.

There are three reasons for this timidity. There is certainly, to some extent, a lack of communication between theoreticians and practitioners. Then, with game computation dominated by image synthesis, there is little remaining capacity for the calculation of AI algorithms. Finally, the game designers do not want to take the risk of relying on methods which are too complex to master. A simple method which satisfies the objectives of gameplay and which is easy to test has their preference.

Some AI tools provide functionality that allows you to build scripted AI at a higher level than a local decision scheme. For example, the SpirOps editor that will be used by Ubisoft in forthcoming games is an editor that relates perception and decision using building blocks. Some blocks are provided in the tool, but the user is able to define new functions and even use advanced AI techniques, like decision algorithms.

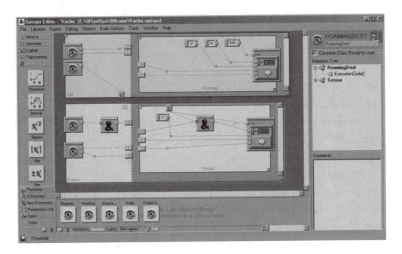

SpirOps editor.

Some games are trying to use more advanced decision techniques based on learning theory which has already been used in many other fields besides game. The game has to learn progressively which decisions are good and adapt its behavior. For example, neural networks use complex networks of small basic decision units whose decisions parameters (a threshold, for example) evolve with the learning process. The creatures of the game *Black & White*, for example, learn their behavior from the player using a simple neural network.

We think that these techniques will evolve in the decade to come, partly as a consequence of improvement in the capabilities of game consoles and partly thanks to the possibilities for experimentation provided by online games.

Present research in AI draws a good part of its inspiration from games. A major school, combining the research contributions coming from narrative theory, psychology, and specification methods, will perform work on the problems tied to interactive narration. In pure AI, we may mention, on the one hand, research on intelligent agents, for the creation of NPC's which have believable behavior (suitable reactions to their environment) and generated emotions, and, on the other hand, the generation of gameplay mechanisms through emergence (artificial life, economic simulation, ecological simulation, etc.).

From our point of view, this evolution will not be used mainly to create autonomous NPC's. Such a goal is very difficult in general and may not be so useful in games. AI will be used to learn and understand the behavior of the player(s) and to adapt the gameplay, the interactive storytelling, and other aspects of the game to the player's expectation. From this point of view, the perception functions will become more complex: the player state must be analyzed though his actions but also through other data coming from sensors like cameras or microphones recording the player's behavior. More complex interfaces, intelligent objects, can also be used (see the end of this chapter). So, perception will rely not only on the state of the virtual world but also on the state of the real world. The decision function will be directly related to the gameplay goals. For example, a believable character is not a character that behaves like a human but a character that fulfils the credibility needs of the player in this given state of the game. This evolution will come from research combining sociology, cognition, interactive narration, and AI. If it is successful, it will have much wider applications than just games.

Game Engines

The figure on the following page is a schematic of the different layers of software and hardware that are part of a video game.

At the highest level, one finds game programming in the form of a script. God advances two units to the right, waits for an event, and then gets angry. The next level involves modeling of the behavior of game objects: what is God and his anger? The following level describes the interface with a generic game engine (or game middle-

ware). This offers a programming interface allowing for the performance of functions common to all games: real-time synthesis of images and sounds, artificial-intelligence algorithms, simulation of physical processes, network game protocols. Unreal engine, Torque Game
Engine (GarageGames), RenderWare (Criterion), NEL (Nevrax), Jupiter
(Touchdown Entertainment), Havok, and Virtools are commercial engines that accomplish some or all of these functions.

As we have already emphasized, the development of these engines
is an essential element in the future evolution of video games. They
facilitate game portability (between different consoles, for example) and
separate the part of game production that comes from basic technology
from that of the development of content, which lies closer to the crafts
of audiovisuals and film.

Technologies of Network Games

Introduction

Network games probably constitute one of the most complex applications of all that is presently envisaged on the Internet and its future
extensions. Let's consider some of the network applications of real-time
cooperation: a game in a room or, more generally, one operated by a
private community, brings together at any given instant about twenty
players at most. This is also the case for a collaborative work system for
computer-airplane design (Constantini, 2001), for an online tutorial,
or for a distributed concert (Bouillot, 2002). The virtual counterpart of
a classroom could accommodate a few hundred students, offering some
limited form of interaction between the teacher and his class. A visit to
a virtual museum or artistic installation would attract an audience of the
same order of magnitude. A typical persistent network game, at present,
attracts a few thousand participants playing simultaneously in a match.
Such a community is envisaged to have more than a million subscribers,
for the games which are available today (*Star Wars, The Sims, World of
Warcraft*). If one considers that 15% to 20% of these subscribers could
be playing simultaneously on the same copy of the virtual world, one
ends up with a total of 200,000 players.

Nevertheless, it is necessary to ask ourselves about the usefulness of
uniting a virtual community of many thousands of people. Outside of

Architecture Level					Examples
Level Design Script Editors					God.move(right, 2);Wait_Event; On button.click
					God_Anger:=new(thunder) God_Anger.lightning, God_Anger.sound
Game Classes					class thunder methods: lightning , sound
General Game Engines					Create_new_object(God, god_geometry.vrml, god_texture.gif,god_voice.wav)
Graphics Engine	Sound Engine	Physics Engine	AI Engine	Network Engine	
General Multimedia API (Application Program Interface) (Direct X, Open GL, Open AL....)					GlMatrixMode(); alsourceplay(source1)
Operating System					Windows, PS2 Monitor...
Hardware					PC, PS, GameCube, XBox
Central Processor, memory, etc.	Graphics Accelerator	Sound Card			

Software and hardware architecture.

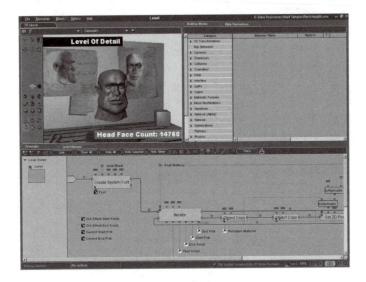

Game programming in the Virtools environment.

the applications coming from broadcast (radio and television), there are few examples of media that put such large groups into play in a continuous relationship. The possible social practices associated with network games must be carefully analyzed if one wants to avoid constructing very complex systems which have no practical interest.

The nature of interactions can be analyzed according to three facets. Does it involve an essentially centralized exchange (from a game manager towards the community) or a localized or generalized open conversation? Further, the constraints imposed by response time and its variability have an important technical impact. In a strategy game like *Starcraft*, a response time of a few tenths of a second is permissible, while it is unacceptable for an adventure or action game like *Counter-Strike*. Synchronized actions, like those involved in a distributed concert (where musicians in different locations play together in real time, using the Internet to exchange the sounds emitted by each instrument) require, besides a response time that is brief on average, a very small variability in this time in order to allow the musicians to settle on a common tempo. Finally, the use of a synchronous exchange medium like voice or video imposes strong psychoperceptive constraints.

Writing and Specification

While general analysis and study of the principles of writing for single-player games has begun to be a subject of research, the design of massively multiplayer games represents a challenge of a different scale. A persistent game, by its nature and economy, has no restriction on its length. The game designer must constantly revive the interest of subscribers by introducing new riddles or mechanisms. This aspect makes it similar to a serial, although one taking place not in episodes, but continuously.

To the conventional component of game design is added the construction of a social universe that, in the simplest case, is of the same order of difficulty as the definition of a new sport, and, in the most complex cases, of a new virtual city. The essential element in this construction is that of giving players the possibility of transforming the game universe at either an individual or collective pace. This principle has already been used in numerous experiments with Internet creation (Balpe, 2000), but an artistic creation may be elaborated without any other constraints than a priori aesthetics, and without any concrete objectives of achievement or interest. This is not the case for games (at least commercial games), whose development must remain controlled. The game designers pose problems to themselves that sociologists and economists are notoriously incapable of solving: what are the types of quests that encourage collective behavior? What are the reward mechanisms that simultaneously interest the player, encourage his improvement, and lead to a stable and just society?

In the field of proactive games, it is necessary to develop a semantic relationship between the virtual universe and the real universe: all or part of our universe interacts with that of the game. This aspect is discussed in the next section.

This writing challenge has a technological counterpart. For the virtual universe to be correctly translated in the game's program—to verify its coherence and follow its evolution in real time—it is necessary to create tools for specification, testing, and maintenance. This is a problem of game engineering or CASE for games, all the more difficult to resolve since it is not currently accurately defined, due to a lack of sufficient experience in the design of such games.

Generativity

The majority of present-day games operate within a predetermined, plot-driven graphic and sonic universe. The scenario is coded in the program, and the graphic and sound components are either symbolic (scene descriptions or MIDI files) or digitally stored (image textures or audio files) data files. Since games are released in DVD-type formats, there is a sufficient memory at one's disposal for storing this information. Interactivity only comes into play upon chaining these elements together and then framing them (through the cameras that are adapted to player movements). This approach has one basic advantage: the designer can retain control over what happens to the player and what he can perceive. There is also, however, a drawback: the limited and repetitive character of the universe produced. Since the lifetime of a game is itself limited, there is an economic compensation for this. To construct a universe that offers constant discoveries for a hundred hours of play is extremely costly, in terms of labor (level designers, graphic artists, musicians, etc.). A persistent universe, having no limit on its lifetime, could thus have infinite cost. Moreover, a very large universe could not be stored in any computer format, especially if it must be periodically renewed. It must then be downloaded through the network, which could pose bandwidth problems for certain components (like the textures).

Another method of proceeding is constructing the universe in a generative fashion. In this case, it is described in the form of behavioral and constructive rules, translated into a program. In general, these rules are local to part of the universe: the behavior of a nonplayer character, the structure of the terrain in the northern mountains, the transition sound when one passes from an urban to a rural zone, etc. The universe is generated in real time as a function of player movement and of artificially created hazards. This dynamic generation instantly creates considerable variations, since it results from all possible interactions between all the rules managing all the objects of the game. The universe thus described represents a very small volume of information, since it is described in the form of a symbolic language. The downside of this choice is the difficulty of predicting, and thus of controlling, a priori, the evolution of the game. Let us give three examples of generative mechanisms, in the areas of artificial intelligence, graphics, and sound.

Numerous behavioral mechanisms for games can be conceived in the manner of simulation of biological or social mechanisms, generally called "artificial life" (Richard, 2003), (Maloron, 2003). A system of artificial life is made up of a collection of rules that guide "intelligent" agents and mechanisms for communication between these agents. By observing the artificial community, constructed in this way with reference to a real community, it is possible to deduce the pertinence of the rules. One of the first applications of artificial life was the study of ant behavior. It is evident that these mechanisms have considerable potential for the construction of persistent games, even if it were limited to giving a less predictable character to the behavior of nonplayer characters. Another very interesting aspect of programming through these agents is that it naturally induces a distributed architecture, by identifying and producing in the code of each agent the objects of the game. This facilitates the determination of which part of the universe should be known to the machine of a given player (see the following section).

A terrain generator is software that constructs an artificial countryside from cartographic rules describing the nature of the country (mountain, plain, etc.) and aesthetic rules (Lecky, 2002). This construction may range from the general form of the terrain (a polyhedric representation of surfaces) to the construction of objects that occupy this countryside (trees, animals, etc.). An "offline" terrain generator creates the terrain once and for all, in the production phase of the game. This terrain is then integrated into the data of the game universe. This technique is already used in the design of present-day games. In the framework of MMOG's, the ambition is rather to generate terrain in real time, that is to say during the course of the game.

Generative music has been experimented with well before its digital treatment (Generative, 2003), in particular for concerts or artistic installations. The formal expression of music and the principles of harmony and counterpoint easily lend themselves to expression in the form of programmable rules. To automatically fabricate music "in the style of Bach" was one of the first sports to which computer scientists devoted themselves. If one moves away from these attempts, whose results are of disputable quality, there are much more successful works, like those of the composer Brian Eno. One way of generating music is to construct agents that interact and generate a MIDI score. This is then played by the synthesizer and a computer. Currently, one finds few games that use this principle, which is certain to have a great future. Nevertheless, the construction of interactive music, such as is presently practiced in games, already poses problems of musical technique (transitions, for example) and digital audio (control over the quality of musical synthesis), but also of control over writing in purely aesthetic terms and image/sound correlation. These difficulties are alleviated in the framework of music that combines generativity and interactivity.

Architecture

The Requirements. A network game is a *distributed computer system*, that is a collection of machines that communicate and develop the computing application (the game) by exchanging messages. This application is made up partly of a collection of static data and programs and partly of the current state of the game. A simple question is posed: what is the best way to distribute information between the different computers? The main objectives of this distribution are that the game is coherent and that the response time to player commands is acceptable. Constraints arise from the bandwidth used by message exchanges, which must be compatible with the amount of bandwidth available to the network, and from the nature of the algorithms executed by each machine, which must be determined as a function of the computational capabilities of the computers.

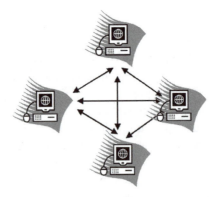

Peer-to-peer architecture.

Games that are played in actual rooms use a local, high-bandwidth network, which allows for the natural transmission of broadcast messages (meaning that a sent message is received by every terminal). The architecture adopted is of the *peer-to-peer* type: each computer sends information on the commands executed by the player to every other computer.

Each computer possesses a complete copy of the game and organizes, based on the information received from the others, its own version of the current state of the game. The great advantage of this type of architecture is the rapid diffusion of commands—a command executed by one player is immediately transmitted to all of the computers in the local network by sending (multiple copies of) a single message.

On the other hand, this solution is of no use on the Internet, even when there is a limited number of players. The delays are too great and too random, and the broadcast of messages is a costly and badly implemented mode of transmission. A solution using peer-to-peer architecture would necessarily lead to incoherent evolution of the game on each computer (see below). In this framework, present-day games use a client/server model. The game is installed on a central machine, the

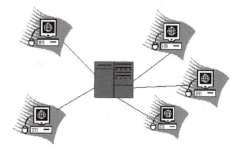

Client/server type architecture.

game server, which receives the commands from the players' terminals. This machine performs nearly all of the necessary calculations (except for certain aspects of the graphics or sound calculations) and returns the results to each of the players' computers. This architecture allows for easier control over the state of the game. On the other hand, it is slower and results in a much larger overall message traffic than peer-to-peer architecture. One needs as many messages as there are participants to broadcast a command.

This solution is applicable to current games on the Internet because they either involve a limited group of players (a closed community of a dozen or so players) or they accept a relatively large response time (on the order of one half-second).

Construction of a Coherent State.   The problem of the construction of a coherent state in a distributed computer system is one of the oldest and most fundamental of the field.   It results from the fact that the propagation time of messages is not definite, that the messages may be destroyed, and that the constituents of the network may break down. By not receiving the same information at the same time and in the same order, two computers may have, at the same instant, a different vision of the state of the game.   Let us illustrate this in the framework of a two-player game.   Alice (A) pursues Bob (B) and must catch up with him. At the initial instant, we suppose that both players have the same

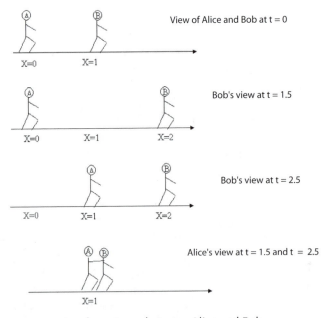

Incoherent race between Alice and Bob.

vision of the state of the game: A is at $X = 0$ and B is at $X = 1$. At the instant $t = 1$, A and B send a command to their respective avatars to advance by one unit. A's command is received by B's computer at $t = 2$, but B's command does not arrive at A (or perhaps only after a very long delay). At instants $t = 1.5$ and $t = 2.5$ each computer recalculates the state of the game. At instant $t = 1.5$, Alice, having not received the command to advance from Bob's avatar, and having advanced her own avatar, deduces that she has caught up with Bob and won the match. Bob, on the other hand, has seen both avatars advance and still believes at $t = 2.5$ that he has not lost.

In this example, we note an important aspect of coherence in games: time management. One of the variables in the game is the *game time*: a game generally has its own clock, which measures the time in the virtual universe. At an instant t (measured in real, absolute time), the current game time could be different for different copies. For all the copies to be coherent, however, they must treat the commands at the same instant as measured in game time.

The same constraint may be found in the area of distributed simulation (IEEE, 1995), (HLA, 2003). However, in a game, which is a real-time interactive simulation, there is a supplementary constraint that the length of time separating two events measured in terms of real time or of simulation time must be nearly identical. In other words, when one simulates an airplane take off for a scientific study, it is permissible for a twenty-minute process to take ten hours of calculation. In a piloting-simulation or a game, this is not possible.

In the majority of computer applications, research into solutions for the problem of coherent states is based on the principle of complete ordering of commands. For example, all of the commands pass through a central server, which assigns them numbers. In a first type of solution, known as "conservative" or "pessimistic," all of the computers that execute the application must perform the commands in the order dictated by the numbering. They therefore all pass through the same steps of the game, with an eventual temporal lag. These solutions may therefore be rather restricted in terms of response time. Indeed, in order to execute a command, a computer must have received and executed all of the preceding commands. In the case where the network has nearly unpredictable transfer delays, and risks message loss, this can be highly penalizing. Another approach, called "optimistic," handles the commands as soon as they are received by a computer and reexecutes the application starting from a coherent situation, if an incoherence happens to be detected.

Neither of these two approaches is sufficient for video games. A video game has a constraint on the response time for certain commands, which results from the necessity for fluidity of the visual and audio animations. Thus, the calculation of synchronized elements (the generation of the framework that puts together the animation and the flow of sound) is necessarily performed on the player's terminal. This may lead one to favor the optimistic approach. However, certain actions must necessarily be perceived in a coherent fashion on all computers. Let us suppose that, on two computers, the position of two objects is not strictly identical. If a player fires at a target, in one case it will seem like the target is hit, in the other that it is missed. Every decision that hinges on the success or failure of this shot will seem arbitrary to one of the two players. In an optimistic approach, one must restart the sequence as soon as the incoherence in the position of the target, and the effect of this incoherence on the shot, is detected. Nevertheless, in order for this operation to be imperceptible, it is only possible to reexecute the game during a very short delay (on the order of a tenth of a second).

Performance. The necessary criteria of performance for the correct execution of a network game are as follows: the rate at which information is exchanged, and the response time between the entry of a command and the materialization of its effect on all of the players' computers.

The problem of transfer rate is perhaps not the most difficult one. On one hand, the bandwidth of Internet connections continues to rapidly improve, with the development of high-speed connections. On the other hand, we have seen that, by using generativity, and, more generally, increasingly advanced compression techniques, it is possible to reduce the volume of information that is transported on the network. This has one drawback: each computer must have the computational means for decompressing the data and generating the behaviors, images, and sound in an amount of time compatible with the constraints of the game.

The transmission delays presently observed on the Internet vary from a dozen milliseconds to a few seconds. Outside of the fact that the higher values are totally incompatible with a reflex game, the great variation in these delays does not allow real interactivity between the players. This problem deals with a number of different aspects, ranging from the development of Internet protocols (Melin, 2003) to the construction of architectures that are effective in terms of the latency of message transmission.

To understand the performance demands created by games, we revisit the classification given by Cronin et al. for an action game like

Type	Example	Class	Comments
Advancing	All avatar movement	RT	The player must see the continuity of all movements
Firing	A bullet or missile is fired	CS/RT	To understand both constraints, one may consider that a targeted player can escape an attack if he reacts quickly enough
Striking	The bullet or missile reaches an object and explodes	CS/RT	
Wounding	An avatar is wounded or killed	CS	To die or come back to life is an important event, but there is time to perform the operation and send out the notices
Rebirth	An avatar comes back to life in a random place in the game	CS	

Table 4.1 Classification of player commands in *Quake* (id Software/ Activision, 1996).

Quake (Cronin, 2001). The authors classify the commands that a player may send according to two criteria: commands that strictly require a short response time (Real Time, RT), and commands which require strong coherence in the state of the game (Consistency, CS). In the first case, image/sound perceptive coherence must be maintained, which implies synchronized refreshment of the image/sound with a latency of less than 100 milliseconds. In the second case, the command induces an event that notably changes the state of the game. CS type commands must necessarily be received and interpreted in the same order on all copies of the state of the game. The more complex commands are those that must respect both criteria. The table at the bottom of the previous pages gives the classification of five types of commands in *Quake*.

Scalability. Scalability is a constraint imposed on network game architecture. It must be capable of dynamically reconfiguring itself as a function of the number of players present. Indeed, if the game meets with a great amount of success, the number of subscribers grows, and the number of players as well. To satisfy their needs, it is thus necessary to make the architecture evolve, while disturbing game function as little as possible. This is a very general set of problems that finds its counterparts in the ensemble of Internet applications (portals, for example).

Fault Tolerance and Security. Fault tolerance is also a classic aspect of distributed computing: the continued rendering of service in the presence of breakdowns of some elements of the architecture. Solutions for fault tolerance rely on a redundancy of hardware and software, with automatic switching during breakdowns. It also requires a coherence between the different copies of the game. Finally, it is necessary to design mechanisms for reinserting the repaired elements without disturbing the game, a problem already mentioned earlier. Among all the computing applications that require fault tolerance, network games are certainly not the most restrictive. Industrial command and control systems are, in fact, much more demanding and complex. There are thus already viable solutions in existence to implement fault tolerance for games, which must be integrated into network game architecture and engines.

Network games, because of both the asocial and game-oriented behavior of certain players and the size of the communities, pose very complex problems of security. It is possible to break down this aspect of the architecture into four classes of objectives:

- player authentification: only authorized people (for example, those who have paid for a subscription) may participate in the game;

- the protection of confidentiality and data integrity against attacks over the network by nonplayers. There are numerous mechanisms which offer some solutions to these two aspects of security problems (Natkin, 2001). They are the subject of numerous developments, since they lie at the heart of electronic commerce;

- control of players' rights over game objects, in order to maintain respect of the rules and to assure the coherence of the virtual world and the virtual society. This is an open research problem in securing cooperative protocols, very difficult at the scientific level, that has numerous facets. It must be resolved in one form or another within the framework of games. There are applications in all sectors of online society: cooperative work, electronic voting, online auctions, etc.

- copyright protection. This is also part of a vast construction zone opened up by the digital diffusion of all media, and in particular by the digitization of film distribution. Numerous techniques are under study, ranging from license recognition (*watermarking*) to the management protocols of distribution rights (*digital rights management*).

Research Examples. We will now look at some research examples in the architecture for computer games.

1. (Semantic Filtering.) As we have already observed, the universe of a game may contain a very large quantity of information. To have a copy of this universe and keep it up to date for each player can be very difficult, even impossible. To send each player a copy of every action by other players is just as imposing. However, this is not necessary; it suffices to maintain that portion of the universe that a player can

observe, and on which he can act. This part of the universe is the *interest area* or *aura* of the player. Moreover, he has no need to receive copies of all the commands within his aura. The true difficulty lies precisely in the aura's determination. This is the objective of semantic filtering (also called interest management).

Semantic filtering starts from a simple point of view: an object may be perceived by a player through seeing or hearing, eventually by touching if a game uses power gloves. The game engine may know perfectly well the ensemble of objects perceptible to a player. This ensemble is called his *focus*. For performance reasons, it is necessary to extend this focus to all of the objects that the player may be able to see after performing a simple action (a slight change of position, for example). A second concept is the space from which an object may be perceived, called its *nimbus*. Simple reasoning leads us to state that one must maintain, in the environment of each player, that portion of the universe that includes his focus and must predict the possible exchanges between two players A and B as soon as the focus of one meets the nimbus of the other. At the most basic level of analysis, it is possible to construct simple solutions based on these concepts and on principles of geographic continuity of the space.

The approach that we have just schematically described only functions in "highly physical" universes, which are constructed according to a simulation of natural laws. This is the case, for example, in sports games. As soon as one considers a universe that is less "down to earth," a basic difficulty arises, which results from the notions of perception and action. The aura of a player is not determined by his physiological perception or what he physically does with his controller but on the virtual perceptions and acting capabilities of his avatar. Nevertheless, in this framework, the possibilities are controlled by the game designer. As soon as he endows a character with a phone, all the players that he may call are in his space of action. Similarly, he may have use of a teletransporter, or a bionic rifle whose scope is limited only by the fantasy of the game. Thus, determination of an aura cannot be based uniquely on geometric considerations. It is based first of all on the principles of gameplay, which determine the space of action for a player and thus its integration into the technical writing tools, determining the aura, nimbus, and focus of each object.

In addition, it is possible in theory to improve this analysis through the training of player behavior. If certain actions are very frequent, the objects that these actions involve must be in the aura. Those that are rarely affected can be included upon event detection. This therefore supposes the introduction within the game of a process of apprenticeship based on artificial intelligence, which is very interesting in principle since it also allows the construction of game rules which are adapted to each player. Currently, this is a difficult research problem.

The optimization of the volume of exchanged messages poses high-level problems of computational protocol. Let us suppose that it were possible to determine at each instant the focus and nimbus of every object. A message that encodes an action by A must be communicated to every object whose focus meets A's nimbus. It is therefore necessary to use a method of communication that sends the messages to a group of subscribers. There are methods in existence, either for the lower levels of telecommunication or for protocols that lie closer to object implementation (object buses), that allow for the production of this type of transmission. For the moment, however, they are not designed for groups whose composition is constantly changing, which is the case for games.

2. (State Prediction—Dead Reckoning). Let us imagine a tennis game on the Internet, based, for example, on a client/server architecture. One of the players hits the ball, which determines its trajectory at the instant that it meets a new object (such as the ground or the racket of another player). The server will therefore apply a simple kinematic model and send to each client the successive positions of the ball at a rate of about thirty times per second. Would it not be more intelligent to leave this calculation to the client terminals, while the server occupies itself with the next collision? Such an approach is called *state prediction* or *dead reckoning*. If this approach is adopted, it is necessary for the server to send out the position at which the collision takes place and the new speed of the ball. This must be done sufficiently early for there to be no discontinuity in the trajectory of the ball and for its motion to seem natural. To make a tennis ball fly backwards would be disastrous.

The effectiveness of this technique has been demonstrated for a common class of objects in network games (and for projectiles in partic-

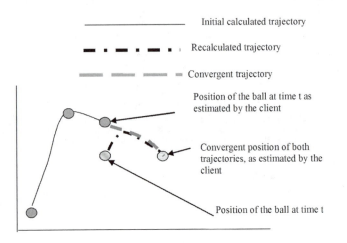

_____ Initial calculated trajectory

▬ ▪ ▬ ▪ ▬ ▪ ▪ Recalculated trajectory

▬ ▬ ▬ ▬ Convergent trajectory

Position of the ball at time t as estimated by the client

Convergent position of both trajectories, as estimated by the client

Position of the ball at time t

State prediction for a tennis ball.

ular), and tends to be implemented in the graphics and physics engines of network games. Like semantic filtering, it is dependent upon the "physical character" of the game rules, which, in this case, limits its applicability.

Technology for Proactive and Ubiquitous Games

At the end of Chapter 3, we presented different classes of games that have at least one of the following properties:

- Proactive. The game interacts with the player's life at uncontrolled times.

- Ubiquitous. The game interacts with the player in nondedicated locations through nondedicated objects or concepts of real life.

- Mobile. The game relies on the player's physical mobility.

These kind of games are the most advanced applications of what is called ubiquitous or pervasive computing.

The current phase of pervasive computing, in which computers are already being embedded in many devices, can be thought of in various ways. We see four major aspects of pervasive computing that appeal to the general population:

- Computing is spread throughout the environment;
- Users are mobile;
- Information appliances are becoming increasingly available;
- Communication is made easier—between individuals, between individuals and things, and between things (Ark 1999).

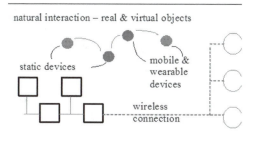

A smart space.

Ubiquitous computing, ubiquitous communication has led to the era of ambient intelligence, with smart spaces characterised by hand-held, wearable, and mobile devices, embedded sensing and communication, and network technologies. Smart spaces may identify and perceive users, their actions, and even their goals, and facilitate their interactions with rich sources of information. Examples of smart spaces are IBM's Dreamspace and Microsoft's Easyliving. These use the concepts of context-aware and location-aware. The captors allow voice, body gestures as inputs. The virtual system tracks all the real contexts in the space, maps the topology of the space (the room) and specifies the tasks (services) for different situations for different users. User's activity and the contents of the space are then recognized by the system. (NDIS, 2005)

The technologies that are used to enrich human interaction with physical/virtual objects and environments have, at the same time, brought about increasingly complex relationships between the real world (RW) and the virtual world VW, in particular, in entertainment applications. (Natkin, 2005)

In the real world, we will find one or several people who know that some of their actions interact with the virtual world. We will call these people the users of the system. This means that users have a representation in the virtual world whose behavior is perceptible to them. This does not always mean that users fully control their representation and, moreover, the influence of their actions on the virtual world.

In classical games, the real world is not affected by the game. In ubiquitous and proactive games, the real world state can be modified in numerous games. For example, in games like *Baufighter* the user's location depends on actions in the game. This feedback relationship is an example of what is called in process control a *reactive system*. The figure on the next page illustrates the feedback loop between the real and the virtual world.

The part of the real world which is affected is the user's physical environment when he is involved in dedicated applications and also all the contextual information needed to interpret the meaning of the virtual world in the user's physical and social context. There are three kinds of real objects that can interact with the game. Some objects are explicitly represented in the system. They can be physical variables like the location of users, the time of the day, or the weather, but they can also be much more abstract elements like the user's emotional state estimated through some biometric measurements, or the value of stock exchange prices received through the Internet. They can also be smart objects like domestic robots whose behavior depends on the game state or even related to other people who are not aware of their interactions with the VW, for example the number of people in a given place at a given time. A second class of objects or hypotheses about the state of

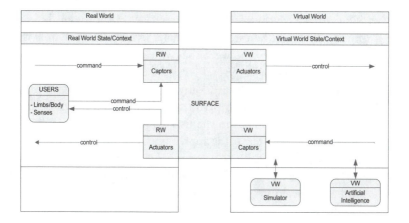

Relationship between two worlds: a reactive system.

the RW are implicitly represented in the game. For example, a game designer may assume that a player who is interested and able to play his game is emerged in the oriental culture and is between 15 and 23 years old. These characteristics are generally not coded in the program but can be found in the system documentation. Finally, some real object of the real world may be affected in a nonpredictable way by the game. For example virtual objects can be sold in the RW through the Internet, which, of course has an impact on the RW economy.

The virtual world is an imaginary space composed of virtual objects governed by simulated physical laws, where the user is represented and where he experiments with the feeling of being present in a virtual environment. The virtual objects may include narrative aspects, perceptual features (graphics and sounds) and actions that can be produced by the object or which can modify the object.

We call the interactive surface the physical materialization of the information which flows from the RW to the VW and vice versa. Four criteria can be used to classify the nature of the surface:

- The surface can be localized in a given place, spread in different locations or be mobile.

- Interactions can be proactive or chosen.

- The surface can be realized in the real world through different means. It might be through standard sensors and actuators that transfer the dataflow between the two worlds. It can be a network of smart objects with several levels of intelligence, according to an increasing order of autonomy. On the one hand, we might have reactive objects that perform dedicated actions whose characteristics may depend on the user context, for example, household or domestic electrical appliances. On the other hand, autonomous objects with their own behavior, using a local AI that includes a perception of the real world, a complex decision system and a physical interaction with the real world may be involved. "Domestic robots," like the AIBO dog of Sony, are typical autonomous systems.

- The ergonomics viewpoint considers the way the objects interact with the user, from a general interface like a PC mouse and screen or the sophisticate interface of the Revolution Nintendo console, to a toy steering wheel in a car, dedicated to car racing games.

Smart autonomous objects are rapidly becoming the interface for many games. Let us take an example taken from research in progress.

> Microsoft's Barney is a plush purple dinosaur that can talk, sing, and play games. Barney can also be controlled by an RF device that plugs into your television set or PC and can pick up instructions striped on the TV signal or encoded in the software to control the child's toy. In many ways, Barney offers even more potential than Barbie since Barney also has input sensors (in his paws and a light-sensor behind his eyes) and can move his limbs (Barney 2004).

The actions (intentional or unintentional) of a child induce various behaviors in Barney: When the child covers Barney's eyes, it plays Peekaboo; if a child shakes one hand of Barney, it plays a game; if two hands are shaken, Barney sings a song; if one hand and one foot are shaken, Barneys goes to sleep (turns off). Barney is a good candidate for the interface of a ubiquitous system: program Barney's memory of events and you get a Tamagotchi and a virtual world state. Add to Barney a learning mechanism which allows it to recognize children (a microphone and a voice authentication system) and analyze its behavior (a simple neural network) and you get a representation of the user. Even if Barney's processing capabilities are not sufficient to implement these functions, Barney can be seen as the interface between the children and a game implemented on a PC, connected to Barney though a wireless network. For such a toy, the user controls the system though his hand and his voice. For example it can be a MMOG for small children, where children do not control their avatars but the avatar of their toys [Natkin, 2005].

The development of this kind of game relies on the evolution of sensors and actuators, networking technology, and several AI concepts.

The ability to integrate low-cost cameras and microphones with an acceptable level of image and sound quality allows the use of sensors in applications for the general public. The most significant examples are the games played using Sony's Eyetoy or the sound interface for Nintendo DS games. Localization of the user is provided in several ways: the analysis of network signals (cell phone, blue tooth, Wifi) or the use of dedicated GPS systems. The impact on the real world and the user, in entertainment, still relies mainly on image and sound diffusion. Interface though more complex devices like smart clothes [Cheock, 2005], toys, and robots are still at the research stage.

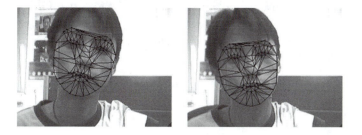

Real-time analysis of a face (Chinese Academy of Science).

The networking revolution is already happening in game devices. WiFi connections are included in the new generation of mobile consoles. Mobile phone games use the actual standard 2.5 GPRS or 3G networks. There are still numerous comparability problems involved

Figure playing with a virtual steering wheel (Chinese Academy of Science).

in designing games to work with mobile devices from several different providers. Very low-level problems are related to the deployment of the new Internet protocol IPV6 and some other networking technology. At an intermediate level, there is a need for a standard interface to program games on various mobile phones.

> Open Mobile Alliance has been launched in 2002. Two hundred companies are member of the OMA: Mobile network operators, mobile phone suppliers, software editors....
> Nokia, IBM, Motorola, Siemens, Intel, Sun for example belong to OMA. The goal of this standardization effort is to ensure a better interoperability and homogeneity between mobile technologies. Among other activities, OMA includes a Game Services working group (OMA GS) to create standard services for mobile based games (Delpiano, 2005).

Higher-level problems, related to cross media platforms, were presented in the previous section.

As games rely not only on the knowledge of the virtual world but also on images, sounds, and other data acquired in the real world, game AI is confronted with the problem of robotic perception analysis, but in general, with less computational capability. This requires advanced signal analysis. For example, using the Eyetoy, you play ball using the head and other limbs of the player.

It means that the image processing system must able to detect the shape and the position of the head in real time. Advanced applications try to understand high-level semantic information, for example, the emotional state of the player from biometric information: his face, his voice and the way he uses his paddle. Once more, we rely on a complex cognition mode of the player embedded in the game.

Research

We have already mentioned the importance of research in the gaming domain. This work, already quite developed in the United States and Japan, is now also becoming more common in Europe. There are many conferences (GameOn, GDC, TIDSE, ACE), and researcher associations are developing (DIGRA, for example).

What does game research consist of? It is not, of course, a fundamental discipline, but rather the emergence of new sets of research problems resulting from game-related applications.

- First, it is indispensable to understand the player both as an individual and as a member of a community. The first theme is thus "sociology and cognition in video games."

- The second theme, *interactive storytelling*, and *ludology* are, in our opinion, the heart of the field. This work covers the convergence of a great number of various aspects, from the theory of narration to that of games, passing through sociological and economic models and the applications of cognitive science, which all contribute to the creation of a video game in all its imaginable forms.

- The third theme, *intelligent games*, introduces study in the areas of artificial intelligence, generative algorithms, management of game objects and software engineering, and narrative requirements for computational equipment.

- This in turn induces both constraints and solutions in the area of architecture of distributed and ubiquitous game engines," which constitute the fourth area of research.

- 5 -

Game In or Game Out

The main goal of this book is to show the importance of video games as a paradigm for the evolution of media and entertainment; I hope I have made the point and convinced the reader. To acknowledge this fact, our society must integrate video games as a new cultural phenomenon at the same level as cinema or television. As we have remarked earlier, games have surpassed movies in economic terms, but they are still frowned upon as a respectable element of popular culture. Establishing their rightful place depends on the development of quality training at all levels of education, the creation of an independent critical analysis of games relying on a living memory of game history, and maybe the emergence of an "art game" genre. In this conclusion, I will focus on two main points: training and art games.

Needs and Pedagogy of Training for Games

When I began to advocate for a school for games, some professionals were not convinced of the necessity for such a school. Numerous universities provided some courses devoted to special aspects of game development, such as programming, graphics and animation, writing and narration. But to my knowledge, there was no specific approach to the teaching of design and development of games anywhere in the world, except for a school in Japan sponsored by the publisher Konami. All of the games produced so far, the great and the bad, have been designed by people trained in various fields, from electrical engineering to cinema and audiovisuals, or simply clever designers without any academic background. Many game designers think that there is no reason to change the system and that academic training and analysis will lead to more conventional games. On the other hand, some publishers and managers of game studios agree that the game design and production world is changing and that a structured and reflective approach will lead to a new generation of games and new applications of game design principles.

The curriculum for the graduate school of games is based on the following assumptions.

- A specific job in the game industry is a specialization of a comprehensive body of basic knowledge.

- The production process of games is closely related to the film production process, a cooperative work in multidisciplinary teams.

Thus, the school offers a European master's degree open to students with a bachelor's degree in at least one of the following fields: audiovisuals, visual arts, sound and music design, computer science, and cognitive science. Students are selected for their background, their creativity, and their passion for video games. The structure of the education is inspired by film schools (FEMIS, INSAS, NYFA, Lodz Film School, etc.). The two main goals of the curriculum are the following.

- To train people in multidisciplinary teamwork according to the processes and the technologies of the game industry.

- To enhance each student's technical knowledge in his/her original discipline (storytelling, audiovisuals, computer graphics, sound and music design, computer engineering) with the concepts, methods, and tools used in the design and implementation of computer games.

Students are accepted in one of six specialties: game design, project management, graphic design, sound design, programming, and man-machine interface according to the information in the table on the next page.

Students initial domain of formation or experience	Profession in the video Game industry aimed	ENJMIN Specialty
Scenario and scripting (audiovisual), literature, information and communication…	Game Design, Level Design	Game Design
Computer Science	Programmers (basic engine, AI, graphic, sound, physics, network…)	Programming
Music, Sound Engineering, Sound in audiovisuals… With some knowledge on audio numeric	Sound Designer, Composer	Sound Design
Arts, Graphics, Animation, Cinema, photography… with some knowledge on computer graphics	Artist, animators,	Graphic Design
Ergonomic, Psychology, Cognition	Interface Design, Game Evaluation and Testing,	Ergonomic and Man Machine Interface
All previous backgrounds and a good knowledge on economy, accounting and marketing	Project Manager, Editor	Process management

The master's curriculum is made up of courses, conferences (seminars), and projects that allow students to do the following.

- Discover the world of video games: history, vocabulary, economy, methods, and production processes.

- Know the basis of the profession of the other participating parties in the conception of a game to be able to work together. For example, we teach the basics of programming and computer graphics to a sound engineer.

- Learn, by domain of specialty, the methods and the technologies used today and those planned for tomorrow in the development of video games.

- Experience the multidisciplinary game-design process. In particular, a group of nine students with a given proportion of all specialties has to complete the preproduction phase of a game within a six-month period. The result must include the game design, the graphic and sound design, the interface, the software architecture, the validation plan, the planning, and an evaluation

Kitchen Frenzy (the author and ENJMIN, 2005).

of the production costs. A prototype of the game is realized using industrial design tools for games.

- Gain experience in his future profession in a four- to six-month internship in the industry.

This curriculum has been developed because it breaks down barriers between the different domains and leads to a less complex and less expensive production process. But the creation of great graphics or an efficient game architecture requires very different basic knowledge and focus. You may sometimes find people having both skills, but it is an exception. Starting from the same viewpoint, more and more institutions in Asia, America, and Europe are developing undergraduate and graduate degree program (see http://www.gamasutra.com/education/).

Art and Games

The perception of games as an original art form is controversial and illustrates the differing points of view about games in our society. Due to their wide distribution, games are considered mass-market enter-tainment products, which does not mean that some games cannot be considered pieces of art. Some films have been widely distributed and are clearly cinematic masterpieces (think of David Lynch's *Mulholland Drive* as a significant example). All the characteristics of games can be found in various genres of art: audiovisuals in cinema, interactiv-ity in music and fine arts, social interactions in performances. There are already numerous artists who have designed works based on game technology. For example, several installations of Web art use the level editor from a game to build a new game with an aesthetic point of view. Kolkoz (http://www.galerieperrotin.com/boutique_multiple.php) in the installation "kolkoz.org video game," used a Quake editor to create a virtual reproduction of an art collector's apartment. Each virtual apart-ment includes the furniture and works of art of the collector and even avatars of the collector and his friends. The "player" can walk through the apartment but can also take his gun and shoot everything. This work and other pieces based on the same principle have been shown as installations in art galleries and exhibitions (see http://en.wikipedia.org/Artistic_computer_game_modification). These are certainly works of art, but they can be considered more like "art about games" than game art, in the same way that many pieces of the early period of Nam June Paik are more works of art whose subjects are television and video media.

Machinima movies (http://www.machinima.org/) are also a way to use games to produce animated films in general and art movies in partic-ular. A machinima movie is an animation that is produced by recording a game session. Some games (like *The Movies* or *The Sims 2*) have in-corporated tools for producing machinima. Plug-ins and other kinds of recording tools have been developed to produce machinima from stan-dard game engines. Machinima is by itself a new media universe, and, like the video revolution in the eighties provides a way to produce low-cost films, machinima is a way to produce low-cost animations and to distribute them over the Internet. Of course, there are a great variety of machinima movies, from virtual documentaries (*The French Democracy*) to virtual TV series (*Black and Blue*). Machinima is certainly a new way to produce works of art, but in its form, it is not fundamentally different from 3D animation.

Kolkoz avatars in Kolkoz.org video games.

Many artists and critics claim that games are a new art form. Tiffany Holmes (Holmes, 2003) gives the following definition of art games: "[A]rt games contain at least two of the following: a defined way to win or experience success in a mental challenge, passage through a series of levels (that may or may not be hierarchical), or a central character or icon which represents the player."

Nic Kelman (Kelman, 2004) proposes a "video-games art manifesto" with the following sentence: "The interactivity of games provides them with a unique potential to connect with their audience, possibly more deeply than any established art form. Recognizing that the interaction creates a stronger emotional bound between player and character or between viewer and character or reader and character is essential for the medium breaking its current bond. It is time this bond was exploited to generate a wider range of emotions than merely intense excitement."

The two preceding statements point out what is, from my point of view, the fundamental originality of games: a game is designed for a given player, and the core technique of game design is the anticipation of the player's psychology. Game art should rely on this foundation, which is not, for example, the case with most interactive art installations. The installation is an a priori proposal made by the artist. Its reception by the public is then analyzed by the artist or the critic. This gives us some indication of what might differentiate a work of "game art," but it does not define how and when video games can be considered as a new art form.

In a very interesting paper, Eric Leja (Leja, 2005) analyzes this problem from a sociological point of view. He gives answers to the following three questions.

- Are video games eligible to be called works of art? "Yes, a video game may contain art and express an artistic sensibility by its own structure."

- Are game developers eligible to be called artists? "Yes, the whole development team is eligible to the artist status... Moreover, in certain cases, the player itself is eligible to this status."

- Is the video game a new art genre? "Yes, but it needs to be socially recognized in this status."

Details of the analysis can be found in the paper, but the notion of social recognition must be considered in further detail. A way to analyze this problem is to consider games either as the child of cinema or of television (Natkin 2005). The social recognition of the cinema as an art genre is indisputable. One of the main justifications for this recognition is the existence of a living memory of the history of cinema: everybody can see an old film of Charlie Chaplin, and the work of Alfred Hitchcock is constantly revisited by critics and in film schools. In contrast, the history of television is left to the experts, and new production rarely refers to a historical aesthetic viewpoint. Television is not generally considered an art form, but this has not always been the case. Dieter (Dieter, 2004) shows the progressive divergence between television and the art scene, leading to the final equation $VT \neq TV$: video art is different from TV. From this historical viewpoint, if we consider online games to be the future of broadcast media, the chance to see the birth of game art seems to be small. This conservative viewpoint may, however, be modified: online games provide a new method of creation, like video, but also a new method of distribution. So, to paraphrase Joseph Beuys, anybody may become a game artist. Art movies are a small market, but it is the main genre in which the cinema renewed its inspiration. The birth of art games relies on the birth of alternate production systems, alternative funding, and the appearance of a new generation of game designers with provocative ideas.

Bibliography

[1] D. Adams. "The Majestic Beta Plays Us, and We Live to Tell the Tale." Available online (http://pc.ign.com/articles/128/128565p1.html), 2001.

[2] T. Akenine-Möller and E. Haines. *Real-Time Rendering*, Second edition. Natick, MA: A K Peters, Ltd., 2002.

[3] T. Alexander, ed. *Massively Multiplayer Game Development*, Game Development Series. Hingham, MA: Charles River Media, 2003.

[4] M. V. Aponte, Y. Lyhaoui, and S. Natkin. "Game Analysis of Attacks on Online Games." In *Proceedings of CGAIMS05*, edited by Q. Mehdi, N. Gough, A. Elmaghraby, D. Jacobi, and D. Anderson. Los Alamitos, CA: IEEE Press, 2005.

[5] W. S. Ark. "A Look at Human Interaction with Pervasive Computers." *IBM Systems Journal* 38:4 (1999), 504–507.

[6] C. Bailblé. "La perception et l'attention modifiées par les dispositifs du cinema." Doctoral thesis, University of Paris VIII, 1999.

[7] J.-P. Balpe. *Le contexte de l'art numérique.* Paris: Hermès, 2000.

[8] P. Bettner and T. Terrano. "1500 Archers on 28.8: Network Programming the Age of Empire and Beyond." Available online (http://www.gamasutra.com/features/20010322/terrano_01.htm), 2001.

[9] B. Book. "These bodies are FREE, so get one NOW!: Advertising and Branding in Social Virtual Worlds." Available online (http://papers.ssrn.com/sol3/papers.cfm?abstract_id=536422), 2004.

[10] N. Bouillot. "Métaphore de l'orchestre virtuel, étude des contraintes système et résau puis prototypage." Report of session DEA SIR. Paris: CNAM, 2002.

[11] E. Castronova. "Blizzard Goes to War." Available online (http://terranova. blogs.com/terra_nova/2004/12/blizzard_goes_t.html), 2004.

[12] G. Cato. "MMOs: It's the Economy, Stupid." Available online (http:// overanalyzed.com/printview.php?t=19&start=0), 2004.

[13] A. D. Cheok, K. H. Goh, W. Liu, F. Farbiz, S. W. Fong, S. L. Teo, Y. Li, and X. Yang. "Human Pacman: A Mobile, Wide-Area Entertainment System Based on Physical, Social, and Ubiquitous Computing." *Personal and Ubiquitous Computing* 8:2 (2004), 71–81.

[14] M. Chion. *Un art sonore, le cinéma: Histoire, esthétique, poétique*, Cinémas Essais. Paris: Cahiers du Cinéma, 2003.

[15] F. Constantini, C. Toinard, N. Chevassus, and F. Gaillard. "Collaborative Design Using Distributed Virtual Reality Over the Internet." In *Proceedings SPIE Internet Imaging*. Springfield, VA: SPIE, 2001.

[16] P. Cook. *Real Sound Synthesis for Interactive Applications*. Natick, MA: A K Peters, Ltd., 2002.

[17] A. Cronin, B. Filstrup, and A. Kurc. "A Distributed Multiplayer Game Server System." UM EECS589 Course Project Report. Available online (http://warriors.eecs.umich.edu/games/papers/quakefinal.pdf), 2001.

[18] Defense Modeling and Simulation Office. "High Level Architecture." Available online (https://www.dmso.mil/public/transition/hla/ index_html), 2003.

[19] R. Demaria and J. L. Wilson. *High Score! The Illustrated History of Electronic Games*. Berkeley, CA: McGraw-Hill Osborne Media, 2003.

[20] J. Dupire, A. Topol, and P. Cuband. "Using Game Engines For Non 3D Gaming Applications." In *Proceedings of CGAMES05*, edited by Q. Mehdi, N. Gough, and S. Natkin, pp. 304–307, Los Alamitos, CA: IEEE Press, 2005.

[21] A. Duvillier. "Le net art bouleverse-t-il le champ de l'art contemporain?" Available online (http://www.artemis.jussieu.fr/hermes/hermes/ actes/ac0102/netart_duvillier.htm), 2002.

[22] D. Elektro. "Preview: 'Majestic' Online Game Blurs Reality." Available online (http://www.cnn.com/2001/TECH/computing/01/08/ majestic.idg/index.html), 2001.

[23] A. Favier. "Les MMORPG modèles des Places de Marché." Available on-line (http://www.univ-nancy2.fr/COLLOQUES/METAMORPHOSE/communications/Allal-Cherif-Favier.pdf), 2004.

[24] F. Fries. "Propositions pour développer l'industrie du jeu vidéo en France." Report to the attention of Mr. Francis Mer, Minister of Economy, Finances, and Industry, and of Ms. Nicole Fontaine, State Minister of Industry, Paris, December 2003.

[25] V. Gal, C. Le Prado, S. Natkin, and L. Vega. "Writing for Video Games." In *Proceedings of VRIC 02*, 2002.

[26] V. Gal, C. Le Prado, J.-B. Merland, S. Natkin, and L. Vega. "Processes and Tools for Sound Design in Computer Games." In *Proceedings of ICMC*, 2002.

[27] Generative. Available online (http://www.generative.net/), 2003.

[28] S. Genvo. *Introduction aux enjeux artistiques et culturels des jeux vidéo.* Paris: L'Harmattan, 2003.

[29] A. Glassner. *Interactive Storytelling: Techniques for 21st Century Fiction.* Natick, MA: A K Peters, Ltd., 2004.

[30] Graoum E., "Le jeu vidéo est-il un art?" Available online (http://www.jiraf.org/files/jv_art.pdf), 2004.

[31] C. Greenhalgh and S. Benford. "MASSIVE: A Distributed Virtual Reality System Incorporating Spatial Trading." In *Proceedings of 15th International Conference on Distributed Computing Systems*, pp. 27–34. Los Alamitos, CA: IEEE Press, 1995.

[32] M. Griffiths and M. Davies. "Does Video Games Addiciton Exist?" In *Handbook of Computer Game Studies*, edited by J. Raessens and J. Goldstein, pp. 359–372. Cambridge, MA: The MIT Press, 2005.

[33] S. Grünvogel, S. Natkin, and L. Vega. "A New Methodology for Spatiotemporal Game Design." In *Proceedings of CGAIDE04*, edited by Q. Mehdi and N. Gough, pp. 109–113. Los Alamitos, CA: IEEE Press, 2004.

[34] E. Guardiola. *Écrire pour le jeu.* Paris: Dixit, 2000.

[35] K. Harland. "Composing for Interactive Music." Available online (http://www.gamasutra.com/features/20000217/harland_pfv.htm), 2000.

[36] T. Holmes. "Arcade Classics Spawn Art? Current Trends in the Art Game Genre." Available online (http://hypertext.rmit.edu.au/dac/papers/Holmes.pdf), 2003.

[37] D. Ichbiah, *La saga des jeux vidéo—De Pong à Lara Croft*. Paris: Vuibert, 2004.

[38] IEEE Computer Society. "IEEE Standard for Distributed Interactive Simulation, Application Protocols (IEEE, 1278.1–1995)," Available online (http://standards.ieee.org/catalog/olis/compsim.html), 1995.

[39] "Soluce complète Homeworld 2." Supplement to *Joystick*, 2003.

[40] L. Julier. *Les sons au cinéma et à la télévision*. Paris: Armand Colin, 2001.

[41] J. Juul. *Half-Real: Video Games between Real Rules and Fictional Worlds*. Cambridge, MA: The MIT Press, 2005.

[42] J. Juul. "The Open and the Closed: Games of Emergence and Games of Progression." In Frans Mäyra, *Computer Games and Digital Cultures Conference Proceedings*, edited by F. Mäyrä, pp. 323–329. Tampere, Finland: Tampere University Press, 2002.

[43] J. Juul. "Working with the Player's Repertoire." Prix des jeunes chercheurs. Imagina, 2004.

[44] D. Kaufman, L. Sauve, and A. Ireland. "Simulation and Advanced Gaming Environments: Exploring their Learning Impacts." In *Proceedings of CGAMES05*, edited by Q. Mehdi, N. Gough, and S. Natkin, pp. 16–25, Los Alamitos, CA: IEEE Press, 2005.

[45] M. Kaminsky, P. Dourish, K. Edwards, A. LaMarca, M. Salisbury, and I. Smith. "Exploring Software Tools for Programmable Embodied Agents, or Hacking Microsoft Barney." Available online (http://www.geekchic.com/~jpd/barney/), 1999.

[46] N. Kelman. "Yes, But Is It a Game." In *Gamers: Writers, Artists, and Programmers on the Pleasures of Pixels*, edited by S. Compton, pp. 225–238. New York: Soft Skull Press, 2004.

[47] S. Kent. *The Ultimate History of Video Games*. New York: Prima Publishing, 2001.

[48] C. Kintzig, G. Poulain, G. Privat, and P.-N. Favennec, eds. *Communicating with Smart Objects: Developing Technology for Usable Pervasive Computing Systems*. London: Kogan Page Science, 2003.

[49] R. Koster. "Economy Stats." Available online(http://starwarsgalaxies. station.sony.com/en_US/players/content.vm?page=Economy%20Stats

[50] J. Kücklich, "Forbidden Pleasure: Cheating in Computer Games." Article submitted to the prix des jeunes chercheurs. Imagina, 2004.

[51] A. Le Diberder. "Histoire des jeux vidéo." Available online (http://deptinfo.cnam.fr/Enseignement/DESSJEUX/infoeleves/ Histoirejeux.pdf), 2003.

[52] A. Le Diberder A. and F. Le Diberder. "La création de jeux vidéo en France en 2001." Ministry of Culture and Communication, *Bulletin du département des études et de la prospective*. Available online (http://www. culture.gouv.fr/dep/), 2001.

[53] A. Le Diberder and F. Le Diberder. *L'univers des jeux vidéo*. Paris: La Découverte, 1998.

[54] G. W., Lecky-Thompson. *Infinite Game Universe, Volume 2: Level Design, Terrain, and Sound*, Advances in Computer Graphics and Game Development Series. Hingham, MA: Charles River Media, 2002.

[55] O. Lejade. "Le business model des jeux massivement multijoueurs et l'avenir des communautés on line." In *Communication aux emagiciens*, 2002.

[56] Lyon Biennial, presentation of artists selected by Laurence Dreyfus. Available online (http://www.biennale-de-lyon.org/bac2001/fran/movie. swf), 2001.

[57] S. Maloron and C. Lattaud. "Vie Artificielle." Available online (http:// www.math-info.univ-paris5.fr/~latc/va/va.html), 2003.

[58] J. L. Melin. *La qualité de service sur IP*. Paris: Eyrolles, 2003.

[59] J.-C. Mézière and P. Christin, *Métro Châtelet direction Cassiopée, Valérian agent spatio-temporel*. Paris: Dargaud, 1980.

[60] S. Natkin. "Architectures et technologies informatiques pour jouer à un million de joueurs." *Les cahiers du numérique* 4:2 (2003), 15–36.

[61] S. Natkin. "Computer Games: A Paradigm for New Media and Arts in the XXI Century." In *Proceedings of Game-On*, pp. 13–19. Ghent-Zwijnaarde: Eurosis, 2003.

[62] S. Natkin. "Les jeux de demain: télévision ou cinéma interactif?" In *Le game design de jeux vidéo: Approches de l'expression vidéoludique*, edited by S. Genvo. Paris: L'Harmattan, 2006.

[63] S. Natkin. *Les protocoles de sécurité de l'Internet*. Paris: Dunod, 2001.

[64] S. Natkin and C. Yan. "Analysis of Correspondences Between Real and Virtual Worlds in General Public Applications." In *Proceedings of CGIV05*, edited by M. Sarfraz, Y. Wang, and E. Banissi, pp. 323–332. Los Alamitos, CA: IEEE Press, 2005.

[65] Natural Digital Interface System, Proposal to the presence ECC FP6 call. CEDRIC/CNAM internal report, 2005.

[66] R. Pellerin F. Delpiano, F. Duclos, E. Gressier-Soudan, and M. Simatic. "GASP: An Open Source Gaming Service Middleware Dedicated to Multiplayer Games for J2ME Based Mobile Phones." In *Proceedings of CGAMES05*, edited by Q. Mehdi, N. Gough, and S. Natkin, pp. 75–82, Los Alamitos, CA: IEEE Press, 2005.

[67] P. Pizer. "Social Game Systems: Cultivating Player Socialization and Providing Alternate Routes to Game Rewards." In *Massively Multiplayer Game Development*, Game Development Series, edited by T. Alexander, pp. 427–441. Hingham, MA: Charles River Media, 2003.

[68] M. Prensky. *Digital Game-Based Learning*. New York: McGraw-Hill, 2000.

[69] J. Printz. *Le génie Logiciel*, Que sais-je? Paris: Presses Universitaires de France - PUF, 2002.

[70] S. Rabin, ed. *AI Game Programming Wisdom*. Hingham, MA: Charles River Media, 2002.

[71] J. Reynolds. "Team Member AI in an FPS." In *AI Game Programming Wisdom 2*, edited by S. Rabin, pp. 207–216. Hingham, MA: Charles River Media, 2004.

[72] N. Richard, P. Codognet, and A. Grumbach. "Créatures virtuelles." *Technique et Science Informatiques (TSI)*, special edition "Vie artificielle." Paris: Hermès, 2003.

[73] A. Rollings and D. Morris, *Game Architecture and Design*, Second edition. Indianapolis: New Riders, 2003.

[74] K. Salen and E. Zimmerman. *Rules of Play: Game Design Fundamentals*. Cambridge, MA: The MIT Press, 2003.

[75] D. Sanchez-Crespau. *Core Techniques and Algorithms in Game Programming*. Indianapolis: New Riders, 2003.

[76] a. P. Saygin, I. Cicekli, and V. Akman. "Turing Test: 50 Years Later." *Minds and Machines*, 10:4 (2000), 463-518.

[77] B. Seys. "Place et rôle des usages des jeux vidéo et d'Internet dans la souffrance psychologique." *Les cahiers du numérique* 4:2 (2003), 117–134.

[78] J. Smed, T. Kaukoranta, and H. Hakonen. "Aspects of Networking in Multiplayer Computer Games." In *Proceedings of International Conference on Application and Development of Computer Games in the 21st Century*, edited by L. W. Sing, W. H. Man, and W. Wai, pp. 74–81. 2001.

[79] P. Spronck. "Online Adaptation of Game Opponent AI in Simulation and in Practice." In *Proceedings of the Game-On Conference*. Ghent-Zwijnaarde: Eurosis, 2003.

[80] SquareSoft. *Final Fantasy X: The Official Strategy Guide*. Honolulu: SquareSoft, 2002.

[81] N. Szilas. "A New Approach for Interactive Drama: From Intelligent Characters to an Intelligent Virtual Narrator." In *Proceedings of the Spring Symposium on Artificial Intelligence and Interactive Entertainment*. Stanford, CA: AAAI Press, 2001.

[82] F. D. Tran, M. Deslaugier, and A. Gérodolle. "A Middleware for Multiplatform, Multiplayer Video Games." France Telecom R & D Documentation, 2002.

Glossary

2D games: Games in which player vision (the virtual camera controlled by the player) of the game universe is limited to a space of two dimensions, which is generally flat.

3D games: Games in which player vision (the virtual camera controlled by the player) of the game universe is a three-dimensional space. The player may, for example, move around an object to see it from all sides.

3D sound: Techniques for recording, synthesis, treatment, and reproduction of sounds that allow one to take into account their positions in space. Not to be confused with stereo sound, which manages sounds within a 2D plane.

action games: Games whose basic focus is player dexterity.

action/adventure games: Adventure games where the principal obstacles that oppose player progress are connected to action sequences (combat, in general).

adventure games: Games for which the narrative web is an essential element of the game's focus. The rules necessarily guide the player through this web.

arcade games: Games that are played in a public place (a game arcade) on dedicated machines, where players pay for each match. Arcade games are generally action games, taking into account the time limit of a few minutes per match.

alternate-reality games: Multiplayer games that are played in real life, generally using the idea of a puzzle that has to be solved with clues that can be found on the Internet. Players communicate through chats and email. These games are often supported by advertising and do not cost anything to play.

augmented-reality games: Games played in real life using an interface like semi-transparent goggles and headphones that allow the player to perceive and interact with virtual objects immersed in the real world.

artificial intelligence (AI): Branch of computer science that investigates the means for endowing computers with behavior that simulates human reasoning and allows them to adapt to any situation. In video games, artificial intelligence refers to any technique which allows one to give the impression that the computer-controlled behavior (of an NPC, for example) is not overly stupid.

Atari: First major company dedicated to video-game production. It was the main player in the field until the end of the eighties. Present commercial name of the game publisher Infogrames.

audio sound: Digital or analog representation of a sound signal. The contents of a musical CD, an MP3 file, or the signal received by a radio receiver are all audio sounds (as opposed to MIDI sound).

avatar: Game character manipulated by the player, and the player's representative within the game.

boss: A particularly large, repulsive, and dangerous monster, which must be defeated in order to complete a level.

camera: In a video game, the cameras are virtual. They determine the different points of view that a player may have of a scene.

chatroom: Web site and an associated interface allowing for exchanged messages between a group of web users, in real time and in the form of text. Chatrooms are often governed by fairly precise social rules concerning subjects and means of expression. The participants are known under pseudonyms and, more and more frequently, represented by avatars. The use of mobile phones as a chat interface is rapidly developing.

cinematic (cut-scene): In video games, cinematics are non-interactive animations (like small animated films). The longer cinematics serve to explain the context of a game or to present a level or quest to the player. Shorter cinematics serve for transitions in camera control.

client/server (architecture): Mechanism for data exchange in network games in which the game is installed on a central machine, the server, which receives commands from all of the player terminals. This machine performs nearly all required calculations (except certain aspects of the graphics and sound calculations) and sends the results to each computer.

closed-community games: Multiplayer games in which a player has some control over the identity of other players. They know each other either by name or under pseudonyms. Played on a local network or on the Internet.

combo: Name given in fighting games to a combination of attack or defense commands. The discovery of effective combos constitutes an important part of the gameplay of these games.

competitive games: See multiplayer games.

cooperative games: See multiplayer games.

digital rights management (DRM): Security protocol norms proposed to assure the control of copyrights on the Internet.

discovery games: Games that allow, through gameplay based on action, strategy, or, most often, adventure, the presentation of a system of (historical, geographical, ecological, etc.) issues.

first-person shooter (FPS): Action game whose basic focus is the ability to fire various weapons, with the image seen by the player coming from a simulation of what is seen by the character under his control.

first-person or subjective viewpoint: Use of a virtual camera system that allows the player to perceive the game through the ears and especially the eyes of his avatar.

game console: Digital system similar to a computer but dedicated to video games played in a private space. Often uses the television as a peripheral for display.

game design: Step in game development consisting of the definition of the virtual universe and the rules of the game.

game engine, game middleware: Generic software which creates images and sound in real time, simulates physical laws, proposes behavioral models for game characters, manages communication, etc.

game guide: Documentation (booklet or Internet site) giving a recipe which allows effective progress through the game.

gameplay: The rules of a game, including the game objective, principal phases, the type of quests that the player must accomplish, and the gaming mechanisms used (such as revelation of partial objectives, obstacles, and resolution techniques).

games of emergence: Games whose gameplay is based on rules and whose basic focus resides in the complexity of their combinations (as opposed to games of progression).

games of progression: Games whose gameplay is based on a story, in which the obstacles (such as puzzles or action sequences) are presented successively (as opposed to games of emergence).

generativity: Principles and techniques allowing the dynamic generation of an object (text, sounds, images) starting from behavioral and constructive rules translated into a computer program. In games, a generative mechanism may also be interactive and thus depend on the actions of the player.

guild: Association of players acting in concert in MMORPG's who constitute a social group in the virtual universe.

image bitmap: Digital image represented in the form of a table of pixels, which is subsequently compressed. In opposition to vector images, which are a symbolic representation of an image (comparable to the comparison between audio sound and MIDI sound).

immersion: Principles and techniques allowing a player to receive the impression that he fully participates in the game universe. Relies on narration, perception, or gameplay.

interactive music: Music whose evolution depends on player actions.

interactive storytelling: Principles and mechanisms which allow for adaptation of a game's progression, and in particular of the narrative framework, to the behavior of the player.

LAN party: Gathering having as its objective the playing of a competitive game with several players (a dozen at most) in a given place. The computers or consoles are interconnected by a local network (LAN, local area network).

Lara Croft: Adventurer with an advantageous physique. First heroine of video games, in the —it Tomb Raider series of games.

level design: Steps of game production allowing the specification of game levels, through the positioning of objects in the game space, construction of the puzzles that the player must solve, and determination and programming of the abilities of the enemies that he must confront.

localization: Technology of the mobile phone, among other things, that allows one to localize the carrier of a telephone. This has numerous applications, including some that are game-oriented.

localized ubiquitous games: Ubiquitous games that rely on the knowledge of the player's physical location.

Mario: Mustached Italian hero plumber from the game *Donkey Kong*, who became Nintendo's mascot.

massively multiplayer online games (MMOG): Games played with a very large number of players (from a few dozen to a few thousand) in a vast, persistent, virtual universe. These are often role-playing games (MMORPG, massively multiplayer online role-playing games).

mobile games (portable games): Single-player or multiplayer games played on a mobile phone, personal digital assistant (PDA), or portable console. The physical mobility of the player is often an element of the game.

multiplayer games: Games that are played with several players. One may distinguish between cooperative games, where a group of players plays against the computer, and competitive games, where the players play, individually or on a team, against each other. A given game often has both a single-player mode and a multiplayer mode.

multi-user dungeon (MUD): First multiplayer games, played on the ARPANET then on the Internet, developed in the eighties. They allow the player to move via textual commands through a fantasy medieval world.

musical instrument digital interface (MIDI): Norm of symbolic representation of music and musical instrument interactions on networks. For example, a MIDI file may contain commands that signify: play an A, on a violin, for a time t and using a loud attack. This norm, dating from more than twenty years ago, is still evolving, particularly in the MPEG4 format.

nonplayer character (NPC) or bot: Character whose behavior is controlled by the computer (and not by the player).

open-community games: Multiplayer games in which a player has no control over the identity of other players. Generally played on the Internet.

peer-to-peer (architecture): Mechanism of data exchange for network games in which each computer sends the commands executed by the player to every other computer.

persistent games: Games whose states are preserved and that continue to evolve even in the absence of players. The MMOGs are persistent multiplayer games. Simulations of aquariums or other ecological systems and the Tamagotchi (virtual beings which must be taken care of so that they don't perish) may be considered persistent single-player games.

pervasive computing: Similar to ubiquitous computing but with emphasis on the proactive form of the player and the system interactions.

polygons (number of): The structure of a graphic object in 3D image synthesis is made up of an assembly of flat polygons. The number of polygons used to describe an object is a basic component of the quality of visual rendering. It is also an element that influences the complexity of image synthesis, which in (PC or console) games must be done around fifty times per second. One therefore often measures the power of a console by the number of displayable polygons per second.

Pong: One of the first video games. Rudimentary simulation of a tennis game.

proactive games: Games that intervene in an unsolicited way into the everyday life of the player, for example by sending him emails or by calling him on the phone.

puzzle games: Computer imports of "classic" games for several players, in which the computer plays the role of one of the players: for example, Chess, Monopoly, etc. What characterizes these games is the symmetric position of the player and the computer: both know from the beginning the rules that are imposed on them and have a symmetric role.

IRL (in real life): A physical encounter between players, as opposed to encounters through the network.

RPG (role-playing game): Game in which a player controls a character in an adventure. However, the powers of the character, and thus his ability to progress in the adventure, depend on a complex system of management belonging to the mechanisms of a strategy game.

RTS (real-time strategy): See strategy games.

semantic filtering: Mechanism of data exchange in network games that allows a player's machine to maintain only that part of the universe that he can observe and on which he can act.

single-player games: Games that are played by one player against the computer. A given game often has both a single-player mode and a multiplayer mode.

Sonic: Quick-moving hedgehog who is the mascot of Sega, publisher and one-time game console manufacturer.

sound design: Design of the sonic architecture of a game and, more generally, of an audiovisual work. The sound design of a game involves, in general, the choice of sound effects, music, and voices, as well as their organization in time and space in relation to the image.

sports games: Games built around a simulation of an individual or collective sport. These are most often action games, but there are a growing number of sports games that incorporate a strategic aspect: management and coordination of teams, choice of equipment, etc.

state prediction (dead reckoning): Technique of network games consisting of approximating the position of an object by interpolation, in the absence of exact knowledge of this position.

strategy games: Games whose principal objective is the management of a universe. One distinguishes the games where the computer and the player take turns playing and the games in real time (RTS, real-time strategy), where the decision-making process is continuous.

synthesis of images or sounds: Algorithms allowing the fabrication of a visualizable image on a screen or an audible sound through a speaker, starting from a textual description of the visual or sonic scene and the position of observation or hearing. In video games, since the evolution of objects and the position of observation depend on the actions of the player, and since the player immediately perceives the evolution of the scene, this calculation must be done in real time.

texture: Image bitmap that is used as material for covering the surface of a synthesized image. By extension, one uses the same term to characterize an audio sound that serves as a sonic source for an object in a virtual scene. The association of a texture to a scenic element is called texturing.

The Sims: A game that simulates social behavior in an average city.

third-person viewpoint: Use of a virtual camera system that allows the player to perceive the game while looking at his avatar. The camera is generally placed above and behind the avatar.

ubiquitous computing: A technology of distributed computing with intelligent devices that are able to identify and perceive users, their actions, and even their goals, and facilitate interactions with rich sources of information.

ubiquitous games: Games that take place in a mixture of the real world and the virtual world of the game.

video game (computer game): Audiovisual interactive work whose primary objective is to entertain its users/spectators, and which uses for its performance an appliance based on computer technology. The term *computer game* is often used for games played on the computer, and the term *video game* for games played on a console.

watermarking: Collection of digital techniques that allow the insertion of a hidden mark into a digital object, permitting, for example, its creator to be specified.

Index